Grade 3

Scott Foresman

Grammar and Writing Practice Book

D1567787

Glenview, Illinois • Boston, Massachusetts • Chandler, Arizona •
Upper Saddle River, New Jersey

ISBN-13: 978-0-328-38941-4
ISBN-10:   0-328-38941-2

2 3 4 5 6 7 8 9 10   12 11 10 09
CC1

Contents

Grammar and Writing Practice Book

Grammar Cumulative Review

Standardized Test Practice

Unit Writing Lessons

My Writing Checklist

My writing is **narrative.** It has
- ❏ a beginning, a middle, and an end
- ❏ characters
- ❏ a setting
- ❏ a story line

My writing is **descriptive.** It
- ❏ creates a picture of a person, place, or thing
- ❏ uses words that appeal to the senses
- ❏ offers strong details

My writing is **expository.** The information in it
- ❏ is arranged in an order that makes sense
- ❏ includes transition words, such as *first, next,* and *last*
- ❏ has been checked for accuracy

My writing is **persuasive.** It
- ❏ includes reasons for my opinion
- ❏ uses persuasive words, such as *must* or *best*
- ❏ is organized in the order of the importance of my ideas

Grammar
Lessons

Sentences

A **sentence** tells a complete thought. It begins with a capital letter and ends with a punctuation mark. An incomplete sentence is called a **fragment.**

Sentence	The lights go out.
Fragment	Suddenly blink on and off

Directions Write the group of words that is a sentence.

1. The boys make a fort.   Can't play computer games.

_____

2. Played checkers and board games.   Mom tells stories.

_____

Directions Decide whether each group of words is a sentence or a fragment. If it is a sentence, write the sentence with correct capitalization and punctuation. If it is a fragment, write *F.*

3. the doll walks and talks

_____

4. has a battery

_____

5. we play card games

_____

6. with our friends next door

_____

Home Activity Your child learned about sentences. Have your child write two or three sentences about an event at school.

© Pearson Education, Inc.3

Sentences

Directions Add your own words to make complete sentences. Write the new sentences. Remember to use capital letters and punctuation marks.

1. _____ can make the power go out.

_____

_____

2. Toys with batteries _____.

_____

_____

3. Without power, you can _____.

_____

_____

4. _____ are fun to play.

_____

_____

Directions What are some things to do when the power goes out? Write three sentences about fun games or other activities.

_____

_____

_____

Home Activity Your child learned how to use sentences in writing. Have your child write two or three sentences about something he or she saw on the way to or from school.

Grammar and Writing Practice Book

Sentences

Directions Mark the letter of the sentence that has correct capitalization and punctuation.

1. **A** This is my favorite game
    B this is my favorite game?
    C This is my favorite game.
    D this is my favorite game.

2. **A** Did you plug in the computer
    B Did you plug in the computer?
    C did you plug in the computer
    D did you plug in the computer?

3. **A** there is no power.
    B There is no power
    C there is no power?
    D There is no power.

4. **A** We enjoy board games
    B we enjoy board games.
    C We enjoy board games.
    D we enjoy board games?

Directions Mark the letter of the complete sentence.

5. **A** My sister likes arts and crafts.
    B Makes caps and mittens.
    C She and her best friend.
    D Using bright yarns.

6. **A** Reads books about sports.
    B Some books from the library.
    C We read every night.
    D About baseball and soccer.

7. **A** No power in the living room.
    B Dark and gloomy in there.
    C A flashlight in the closet.
    D We need lights for reading.

8. **A** This computer game takes skill.
    B Must move your hand fast.
    C With more practice.
    D Gives hints on playing.

9. **A** A toy firetruck.
    B Makes sounds and lights up.
    C It needs a battery.
    D My brother's favorite toy.

10. **A** A fun card game.
    B She plays cards every day.
    C With her grandma.
    D Deals the cards quickly.

Home Activity Your child prepared for taking tests on sentences. Ask your child to explain the difference between a sentence and a fragment.

Grammar and Writing Practice Book   Unit 1 Week 1   **3**

Sentences

Directions Read each group of words. Write *S* if the group of words is a sentence. Write *F* if the group of words is a fragment.

1. The wind blew all night. _____

2. No power in the morning. _____

3. The alarm clock didn't ring. _____

4. Late for school. _____

5. Fixed the power lines. _____

Directions Decide whether each group of words is a sentence or a fragment. If it is a sentence, write the sentence with correct capitalization and punctuation. If it is a fragment, write *F*.

6. bored and unhappy

_____

7. misses his computer games

_____

8. he finds some old games

_____

9. we play checkers

_____

10. an old board in the closet

_____

Directions Add your own words to make a complete sentence. Write the new sentence. Remember to use a capital letter and a punctuation mark.

11. Computer games _____.

_____

_____

Home Activity Your child reviewed sentences. Say some sentence subjects (*Mom, The boy, Some people*) and have your child add words to make a complete sentence.

Grammar and Writing Practice Book

© Pearson Education, Inc.3

Subjects and Predicates

A sentence has a **subject** and **predicate.** The subject is the sentence part that tells whom or what the sentence is about. All the words in the subject are called the complete subject. The predicate is the sentence part that tells what the subject is or does. It includes a verb. All the words in the predicate are called the complete predicate.

In the following sentence, the complete subject is underlined once. The complete predicate is underlined twice. The verb is circled.

The market (has) many interesting things.

Directions Underline the complete subject of each sentence.

1. Many people buy beautiful carpets at the market.

2. Farmers bring goats to the market too.

3. The vegetables in the stalls look delicious.

4. Children run around the town square.

5. Everything happens at the town market!

Directions Underline the complete predicate of each sentence. Circle the verb.

6. A young boy asks for help.

7. The old man is wiser than the boy.

8. The students in a classroom learn lessons all the time.

9. Animals learn differently from people.

10. My parents teach me many lessons.

Home Activity Your child learned about subjects and predicates. Say a sentence. Have your child identify its subject and predicate.

Subjects and Predicates

Directions Add a predicate to each subject to make a complete sentence. Write the sentence with correct punctuation.

1. A carpetmaker

_____

2. Two goats

_____

3. A merchant in the village

_____

Directions Add a subject to each predicate to make a complete sentence. Write the sentence with correct punctuation.

4. knows many important things

_____

5. builds houses and barns

_____

Directions Think about a lesson you learned when you didn't expect to. Write four sentences that tell about the lesson.

_____

_____

_____

_____

Home Activity Your child learned how to use subjects and predicates in writing. Read a story together. Have your child identify subjects and predicates in story sentences.

Grammar and Writing Practice Book

Subjects and Predicates

Directions Mark the letter of the complete subject of each sentence.

1. Everyone in the world needs something.
   A Everyone
   B Everyone in the world
   C needs
   D needs something

4. People in need ask for help.
   A People
   B People in need
   C ask
   D ask for help

2. A busy carpenter needs tools.
   A A busy
   B carpenter needs
   C A busy carpenter
   D needs tools

5. Someone in the town helps others.
   A Someone
   B town helps others
   C Someone in the town
   D helps others

3. Goats on a farm need food.
   A Goats
   B need food
   C Goats on a farm
   D food

6. Every town needs helpers.
   A town
   B needs
   C Every town
   D helpers

Directions Mark the letter of the complete predicate of each sentence.

7. A wise man lives in the village.
   A A wise man
   B man
   C lives
   D lives in the village

9. The carpenter built a pen for the goats.
   A The carpenter
   B built a pen
   C built a pen for the goats
   D built

8. The farmer keeps goats in the pen.
   A keeps goats in the pen
   B keeps goats
   C The farmer
   D goats

10. The spinner made beautiful thread.
    A The spinner
    B made beautiful
    C made beautiful thread
    D made

Home Activity Your child prepared for taking tests on subjects and predicates. Say a sentence about your family. Ask your child to identify the subject and the predicate of the sentence. Continue with other sentences.

© Pearson Education, Inc.3

Subjects and Predicates

Directions Underline the complete subject of each sentence.

1. A fable tells an old story.

2. Many fables teach a lesson.

3. Some characters take a journey.

4. Wise men are fable characters sometimes.

Directions Underline the complete predicate of each sentence.

5. In one fable, a young boy finds a special bean.

6. A princess finds a prince.

7. A king learns something important.

8. You wrote a clever fable.

Directions Add a predicate or a subject to make a complete sentence. Remember to use capital letters and punctuation marks.

9. A kind merchant in a fable

_____

_____

10. retold fables many times

_____

_____

Home Activity Your child reviewed subjects and predicates. Have your child say sentences about fables and folk tales he or she has read. Discuss the subject and predicate of each sentence.

Name _____

Statements and Questions

A sentence that tells something is a **statement.** It is also called a **declarative sentence.** A sentence that asks something is a **question.** It is also called an **interrogative sentence.**

Statement   The lake has many fish.   **Question**   Did you catch a fish?

A statement begins with a capital letter and ends with a period. A question begins with a capital letter and ends with a question mark.

Directions Write each sentence. Add the correct end punctuation. Write *S* if the sentence is a statement, or declarative sentence. Write *Q* if the sentence is a question, or interrogative sentence.

1. Are the winters long in the Arctic

_____

2. Spring is a good season for fishing

_____

3. We have a good fishing pole

_____

Directions Add one word from the box to make each statement into a question. Write the new sentence. Use correct capitalization and punctuation.

can   will   should   do

4. The people catch fish in the frozen lake.

_____

5. They take them home for a feast.

_____

Home Activity Your child learned about statements and questions. Have your child make up one statement and one question about an animal he or she likes.

© Pearson Education, Inc. 3

Statements and Questions

Directions Use each subject and verb in a sentence. Add words to make the sentence complete. Each item will tell you whether to write a statement (declarative sentence) or a question (interrogative sentence).

Example: Statement: family walks

The family walks to the lake.

1. Statement: fish jump

_____

2. Question: children help

_____

3. Statement: lake freezes

_____

4. Question: men catch

_____

5. Question: people eat

_____

Directions Write three sentences about going fishing. Include at least one question.

_____

_____

_____

_____

Home Activity Your child learned how to use statements and questions in writing. Have your child write a letter to you that includes at least one statement and one question.

© Pearson Education, Inc. 3

Statements and Questions

Directions Mark the letter of the sentence that is written correctly.

1. **A** Is it cold at the lake.
   B The wind blows hard
   C When does spring begin?
   D it is my favorite season?

2. **A** the people eat much fish
   B fish is a tasty meal?
   C they have a big feast.
   D Everyone shares the fish.

3. **A** Did you go fishing?
   B he borrowed my pole.
   C a big fish leaps out of the lake
   D Can I catch it

4. **A** does the lake freeze in winter?
   B Can we skate on the ice?
   C Do fish live in the ice.
   D what kinds of fish live there.

5. **A** I fish in the summer.
   B It's much warmer then
   C the fish bite in the morning?
   D we must get up early.

6. **A** is that your lucky pole?
   B Will you put a worm on the line?
   C Do fish like worms.
   D fish like all kinds of bait?

7. **A** the lake is very quiet?
   B The water looks clear
   C the sun shines brightly.
   D A fish splashes in the lake.

8. **A** Who will clean the fish?
   B is it a messy job?
   C May I help.
   D how will we cook the fish.

9. **A** Arctic winters are long
   B Is life hard in the Arctic?
   C People help one another
   D they catch fish in the spring

10. **A** The fish smells good.
    B Mom cooks it in a stew
    C I put in carrots
    D we eat it in big bowls.

School-Home CONNECTION

Home Activity Your child prepared for taking tests on statements and questions. Read a story together. Have your child identify statements and questions in the story.

Statements and Questions

Directions Write *statement* if the sentence is a statement (declarative sentence). Write *question* if the sentence is a question (interrogative sentence).

1. Kumak took his sled to the lake.   _____

2. Did the whole family go fishing?   _____

3. Who caught the first fish?   _____

4. Everyone pulled on the big fish.   _____

Directions Write each sentence. Add the correct end punctuation. Write *S* if the sentence is a statement and *Q* if the sentence is a question.

5. The people can have a big meal

_____

6. What tastes good with fish

_____

7. Did everyone enjoy the feast

_____

8. The children help clean up

_____

Directions Write a statement about a good meal you have had. Then write a question you might ask someone about a big meal.

9. _____

_____

10. _____

_____

Home Activity Your child reviewed statements and questions. Say *question* or *statement* to your child. Have him or her make up that kind of sentence about a sport.

© Pearson Education, Inc. 3

Name _____

Commands and Exclamations

A sentence that tells someone to do something is a **command.** It is also called an **imperative sentence.** A sentence that shows strong feelings is an **exclamation.** It is also called an **exclamatory sentence.**

> **Command**   Buy some apples.
> **Exclamation** What juicy peaches these are!

Some commands begin with *Please.* Commands usually end with periods. The subject of a command is *you.* The word *you* is not written or said, but it is understood. Exclamations can express feelings such as surprise, anger, or excitement. Exclamations begin with a capital letter and end with an exclamation mark.

Directions Write the sentences. Add the correct end punctuation. Write *C* if the sentence is a command, or imperative sentence. Write *E* if the sentence is an exclamation, or exclamatory sentence.

1. Please get a loaf of bread

_____

2. Wow! This supermarket is huge

_____

Directions Use a word from the box to complete each command or exclamation. Write the new sentence. Use correct capitalization and punctuation.

> What   Look   Talk   How

3. _____ on that shelf for cereal.

_____

4. _____ busy the workers are!

_____

Home Activity Your child learned about commands and exclamations. Have your child make up one command and one exclamation about saving money.

Name _____

Supermarket

APPLY TO WRITING

Commands and Exclamations

Directions Write a sentence for each item. Follow the directions.

1. Write a command that you might say to a family member at the supermarket.

_____

2. Write an exclamation about the fruits at the supermarket.

_____

3. Write a command to a friend at the supermarket.

_____

4. Write an exclamation that shows surprise about something at the supermarket.

_____

5. Write a command that you might use after shopping at the supermarket.

_____

Directions Imagine you are in a big supermarket. Write one command and two exclamations about the experience.

_____

_____

_____

Home Activity Your child learned how to use commands and exclamations in writing. Have your child make up one command and one exclamation that he or she might use while playing a game outside.

© Pearson Education, Inc. 3

Commands and Exclamations

Directions Mark the letter of the answer that best completes the kind of sentence in ( ).

1. _____ a big watermelon that is! (exclamation)
   A What
   B what
   C What.
   D What!

2. _____ get some cheese. (command)
   A Please!
   B Please
   C please
   D please!

3. _____ for some green grapes. (command)
   A Look!
   B look!
   C look
   D Look

4. The bread smells so _____ (exclamation)
   A good
   B good?
   C good.
   D good!

5. _____ the price of tomatoes. (command)
   A check
   B Check
   C Check?
   D check

6. There are so many kinds of _____ (exclamation)
   A soup
   B soup?
   C soup.
   D soup!

7. Please get a box of _____ (command)
   A crackers?
   B crackers.
   C crackers!
   D crackers

8. What a good price that _____ (exclamation)
   A is?
   B is
   C is!
   D is.

9. The checkout clerks work so _____ (exclamation)
   A fast?
   B fast!
   C fast.
   D fast

10. _____ the bags in the car. (command)
    A Put?
    B put
    C Put!
    D Put

Home Activity Your child prepared for taking tests on commands and exclamations. Have your child write a note about a chore to a family member, including a command and an exclamation. Ask your child to identify each kind of sentence.

Grammar and Writing Practice Book

Unit 1 Week 4 **15**

Commands and Exclamations

Directions Write *command* if the sentence is a command (imperative sentence). Write *exclamation* if the sentence is an exclamation (exclamatory sentence).

1. Enjoy your visit to the farm. _____

2. What green fields those are! _____

3. The corn crop is huge! _____

4. Look at the lettuce plants. _____

Directions Write the sentences. Add the correct end punctuation. Write *C* if the sentence is a command and *E* if the sentence is an exclamation.

5. The farm machines are so noisy

_____

6. Walk through the pumpkin patch

_____

7. What a nice pumpkin that is

_____

8. Take it home with you

_____

Directions Write a command you might give on a farm visit. Then write an exclamation you might use on a farm visit.

9. _____

_____

10. _____

_____

Home Activity Your child reviewed commands and exclamations. Have him or her recall some commands and exclamations he or she made during the day.

Compound Sentences

A **simple sentence** has one subject and one predicate. A **compound sentence** contains two simple sentences joined by a comma and a word such as *and, but,* or *or.*

Simple Sentence	I rode my bike to Dan's house.
Simple Sentence	We rode to the park.
Compound Sentence	I rode my bike to Dan's house, and we rode to the park.

Directions Write *S* if the sentence is a simple sentence. Write *C* if the sentence is a compound sentence.

1. Bicycles are important to people in some countries. _____

2. People in some places do not have cars. _____

3. They ride bicycles to work, and they ride them to the store. _____

4. Bicycles cost less than cars, but they are not cheap. _____

5. Bicycles do not make the air dirty, but cars do. _____

Directions Choose one of the words in ( ) to combine each pair of simple sentences. Write the compound sentences on the lines.

6. Chris rode a bicycle up the hill. It was not easy. (but, or)

_____

7. Chris skinned his knee. He bumped his head. (but, and)

_____

8. Now Chris can ride to school. He can ride to the park. (or, but)

_____

_____

Home Activity Your child learned about compound sentences. Say two short, related sentences describing your child. Have him or her combine the sentences to make a compound sentence.

Compound Sentences

Directions Combine each pair of sentences by adding *and, but,* or *or.* Write the
compound sentence. Remember to add a comma.

1. Anya saves money to buy a game. I save money to buy a book.

_____

_____

2. Saving money is hard sometimes. It is worth the effort.

_____

_____

3. Your parents can buy you a bicycle. You can buy it yourself.

_____

_____

4. Save a dollar each week. The dollars will add up.

_____

_____

Directions What would you save money for? Write two simple, related sentences.
Then join the sentences to make a compound sentence.

_____

_____

_____

Home Activity Your child learned how to use compound sentences in writing. Have your child write a
compound sentence about two things he or she learned today.

Grammar and Writing Practice Book

© Pearson Education, Inc. 3

Compound Sentences

Directions Mark the letter of the words that complete the sentence correctly.

1. Ben walked to the _____ rode.
   A game, And David
   B game, or David
   C game, and David
   D game and David

2. There is a path at the _____ is short.
   A park, but it
   B park, But it
   C park, or it
   D park and it

3. You can ride in the _____ can ride on the beach.
   A hills, but you
   B hills, And you
   C hills and you
   D hills, or you

4. Joel's bicycle is _____ is newer.
   A new, or mine
   B new, but mine
   C new and mine
   D new, And mine

5. Skateboards are _____ are fun.
   A fast. and they
   B fast or they
   C fast, and they
   D fast, But they

6. We can _____ can ride.
   A skate, or we
   B skate and we
   C skate, And we
   D skate but we

7. I can go _____ can go slow.
   A fast but I
   B fast, or I
   C fast, Or I
   D fast and I

8. The race was _____ won it.
   A hard. but I
   B hard or I
   C hard and
   D hard, but I

9. Ten people _____ finished.
   A started, Or five people
   B started but five people
   C started, and five people
   D started. and five people

10. Tim parked in _____ parked in back.
    A front, and I
    B front, But I
    C front, or I
    D front and I

Home Activity Your child prepared for taking tests on compound sentences. Have your child find compound sentences in a magazine and identify the two simple sentences that make up each compound sentence and the word that joins the two sentences.

Name _____

Compound Sentences

Directions Write *S* if the sentence is a simple sentence. Write *C* if the sentence is a compound sentence.

1. Katie helps her dad on the farm. _____

2. Katie's dad plants berries, and Katie picks them. _____

3. Sasha's parents own a store, and Sasha helps out there. _____

4. Sasha puts the food on the shelves. _____

Directions Use the word *and, but,* or *or* to combine each pair of sentences. Write the compound sentence.

5. A fair has many things for sale. You can't buy everything.

_____

6. You could buy a toy. You could buy a snack.

_____

7. One stall sells jewelry. Another stall sells hats.

_____

8. Those T-shirts are great. I have many T-shirts at home.

_____

Directions Write two sentences about a fair or an amusement park you have visited. Write one simple sentence and one compound sentence.

9. _____

_____

10. _____

_____

Home Activity Your child reviewed compound sentences. On a walk outside, have your child make up two compound sentences about what you see.

Grammar and Writing Practice Book

© Pearson Education, Inc. 3

Name _____

Penguin Chick

DEVELOP THE CONCEPT

Common and Proper Nouns

A **common noun** names any person, place, or thing. A **proper noun** names a particular person, place, or thing. Proper nouns begin with capital letters. The names of days, months, places, and holidays are proper nouns. Historical periods and special events are also proper nouns.

Common Nouns   You can see penguins at some zoos.

Proper Nouns   On Labor Day, a penguin from Africa was displayed at the New York State Fair.

Capitalize each important word in a proper noun: Fourth of July, Civil War.

Directions Write *C* if the underlined noun is a common noun. Write *P* if the underlined noun is a proper noun.

1. There are not many emperor penguins in our country. _____

2. A sea park in San Diego has an emperor penguin. _____

3. Jon went to the zoo on Independence Day. _____

4. He saw penguins and other unusual animals. _____

5. Whales and penguins are popular sea park attractions. _____

Directions Underline the common nouns and circle the proper nouns in the sentences.

6. It is cold in Alaska on New Year's Day.

7. Penguins do not come from the United States.

8. Seals and polar bears like the cold weather.

9. The Millers will visit Juneau at Thanksgiving.

10. The Iditarod Trail Sled Dog Race is held in March.

Home Activity Your child learned about common and proper nouns. Have your child write the names of friends and family members and explain why the names are proper nouns.

© Pearson Education, Inc. 3

Grammar and Writing Practice Book   Unit 2 Week 1 **21**

Common and Proper Nouns

Directions Rewrite each sentence. Replace each underlined common noun with a proper noun.

1. The city has a zoo with many animals.

_____

2. You can visit the zoo on a holiday.

_____

3. You can see many wild animals at a place.

_____

4. Fish live in a river.

_____

5. There are many interesting animals in that country.

_____

Directions Write a description of a place that has interesting animals. Use at least two proper nouns.

_____

_____

_____

_____

Home Activity Your child learned how to use common and proper nouns in writing. Look at family photos with your child. Have your child write a sentence about a place your family has visited, using at least one proper noun.

Grammar and Writing Practice Book

Common and Proper Nouns

Directions Mark the letter of the sentence that is written correctly.

1. A Kelly went to the zoo in San antonio.
   B kelly went to the Zoo in san antonio.
   C Kelly went to the zoo in San Antonio.
   D Kelly went to the zoo in san antonio.

2. A Those birds nest in hawaii.
   B Those Birds nest in hawaii.
   C Those Birds nest in hawaii.
   D Those birds nest in Hawaii.

3. A New york city has many pigeons.
   B New York City has many pigeons.
   C New York City has many Pigeons.
   D New york City has many pigeons.

4. A The 2000 olympics were held in australia.
   B The 2000 olympics were held in Australia.
   C The 2000 Olympics were held in australia.
   D The 2000 Olympics were held in Australia.

5. A Birds called emus live in that Country.
   B Birds called Emus live in that Country.
   C Birds called emus live in that country.
   D Birds called Emus live in that country.

6. A An eagle flew on the fourth of july.
   B An Eagle flew on the Fourth of July.
   C An eagle flew on the Fourth of July.
   D An eagle flew on the Fourth of july.

7. A Seagulls gathered over the atlantic ocean.
   B Seagulls gathered over the Atlantic Ocean.
   C Seagulls gathered over the atlantic Ocean.
   D Seagulls gathered over the Atlantic ocean.

8. A Amy drew a turkey for Thanksgiving.
   B amy drew a turkey for thanksgiving.
   C Amy drew a Turkey for Thanksgiving.
   D Amy drew a turkey for thanksgiving.

9. A Can birds fly over the washington monument?
   B Can birds fly over the Washington Monument?
   C Can birds fly over the Washington monument?
   D Can Birds fly over the Washington Monument?

10. A The robins sing in April.
    B The Robins sing in April.
    C The robins sing in april.
    D The Robins sing in april.

Home Activity Your child prepared for taking tests on common and proper nouns. On a drive, say the names of things you pass, such as *a street* and *Spring Creek*. Have your child identify which are common nouns and which are proper nouns.

Common and Proper Nouns

Directions Write the sentences. Capitalize the proper nouns correctly.

1. The first zoo in the united states opened just before the civil war.

_____

2. It was the central park zoo in new york city.

_____

3. You can see penguins from antarctica and south america there.

_____

4. Maybe you can go there on presidents' day or columbus day.

_____

Directions Underline the common nouns and circle the proper nouns in the sentences.

5. Many animals at the zoo come from distant places.

6. Koalas come from Australia.

7. Pandas come from China.

8. The aquarium brought some whales from the Pacific Ocean.

9. That beautiful tiger was born in India.

Directions Write a sentence about a wild animal. Use at least one proper noun and circle it. Underline the common nouns.

10. _____

_____

Home Activity Your child reviewed common and proper nouns. On a walk in your neighborhood, have your child name some common nouns and some proper nouns that name neighborhood sights.

Grammar and Writing Practice Book

Name _____

Singular and Plural Nouns

A **singular noun** names only one person, place, or thing. A **plural noun** names more than one person, place, or thing.

Singular Nouns   The <u>boy</u> worked on a farm.
Plural Nouns   The <u>workers</u> picked <u>grapes</u> and <u>onions</u>.

Most nouns add *-s* to form the plural. Add *-es* to a noun that ends in *ch, sh, s, ss,* or *x: lunches, dishes, buses, dresses, boxes.* When a noun ends in a consonant and *y,* change the *y* to *i* and then add *-es: bodies.*

Directions Write *S* if the underlined noun is a singular noun. Write *P* if the underlined noun is a plural noun.

1. Many <u>crops</u> grow in California. _____

2. Workers picked a <u>crate</u> of garlic. _____

3. Farmers need help in their <u>fields</u>. _____

4. Plump purple grapes grow on a <u>vine</u>. _____

5. People buy the <u>fruits</u> at the supermarket. _____

Directions Write the plural nouns in each sentence.

6. The workers loaded boxes of grapes.

_____

7. The trees were full of plump cherries.

_____

8. Mama made tortillas for lunch.

_____

9. Papa picked pears and peaches at the farm.

_____

Home Activity Your child learned about singular and plural nouns. Say "I see a [something in your house]" and have your child say the plural form of the word.

Singular and Plural Nouns

Directions Complete each sentence by adding plural nouns. Write the new sentence.

1. The workers planted _____ and _____ in the field.

_____

_____

2. Mama made a lunch of _____ and _____.

_____

_____

3. You can make a salad with _____ and _____.

_____

_____

4. Papa put fresh _____ into crates.

_____

5. You can buy fresh farm vegetables at _____ and _____.

_____

_____

Directions Write about workers doing jobs on a farm. Use at least three plural nouns.

_____

_____

_____

© Pearson Education, Inc. 3

Home Activity Your child learned how to use singular and plural nouns in writing. Have your child write you a note about his or her favorite meal using at least three plural nouns.

26 Unit 2 Week 2

Grammar and Writing Practice Book

Name _____

Singular and Plural Nouns

Directions Mark the letter of the plural form of the word that completes the sentence.

1. The workers pack _____ of grapes.
   A boxs
   B boxes
   C box
   D boxies

2. Grapes grow in many little _____.
   A bunches
   B bunchs
   C buncheses
   D bunch

3. Some workers pick _____.
   A peachs
   B peachis
   C peaches
   D peachies

4. Crew _____ tell workers what to do.
   A boss
   B bosses
   C bosss
   D bossis

5. Different kinds of _____ grow on the farm.
   A grasss
   B grassies
   C gras
   D grasses

6. Chico had been in many _____.
   A class
   B classs
   C classes
   D classies

7. Students brought their _____ to school.
   A lunchies
   B lunchs
   C luncheses
   D lunches

8. Some people ate _____.
   A sandwicheses
   B sandwichis
   C sandwichs
   D sandwiches

9. Chico read _____ at school.
   A stories
   B stores
   C storys
   D storss

10. Chico could quickly add two _____.
    A number
    B numberes
    C numbers
    D numberses

Home Activity Your child prepared for taking tests on singular and plural nouns. With your child, take turns naming kinds of insects. Have your child write the plural form of each word.

Singular and Plural Nouns

Directions Underline the singular nouns and circle the plural nouns in the sentences.

1. The boy helped his father with jobs on the farm.

2. The man put apples and oranges in crates.

3. Many farmers hired the good workers.

4. Boys and girls learn letters and numbers at school.

5. The boy made a new friend in class.

Directions Write the plural form of the noun in ( ).

6. Big yellow (bus) take the kids to school. _____

7. Chico's dad packed (box) of fruit. _____

8. He has worked in pumpkin (patch). _____

9. The workers do jobs on farms and (ranch). _____

Directions Write a sentence about a job you might do on a farm. Use at least one singular noun and one plural noun.

10. _____

_____

Home Activity Your child reviewed singular and plural nouns. Look at a magazine article with your child. Have your child point out three singular nouns and three plural nouns.

Name _____

Irregular Plural Nouns

A plural noun names more than one person, place, or thing. Most nouns add -s to form the plural. An **irregular plural noun** has a special form for the plural.

    Singular Nouns   A goose and a deer ate a leaf.

    Irregular Plural Nouns Some geese and some deer ate some leaves.

Some nouns and their irregular plural forms are *child/children, deer/deer, foot/feet, goose/geese, leaf/leaves, life/lives, man/men, mouse/mice, ox/oxen, sheep/sheep, tooth/teeth,* and *woman/women.*

Directions Write *S* if the underlined noun is singular. Write *P* if the underlined noun is plural.

  1. The <u>children</u> had a messy room. _____

  2. Aunt Rose would not put a <u>foot</u> into the room. _____

  3. There were <u>leaves</u> on the floor. _____

  4. I've never seen such a sight in my <u>life</u>! _____

  5. <u>Mice</u> could make a nest in there. _____

Directions Write the plural nouns in each sentence.

  6. The men on the farm had a problem.

_____

  7. Deer were eating vegetables from their fields.

_____

  8. The farmers found holes in the lettuce leaves.

_____

  9. The women tried to think of clever solutions.

© Pearson Education, Inc.3

Home Activity Your child learned about irregular plural nouns. Say the words *goose, mouse,* and *child* and have your child say the plural form of each word.

Name _____

Irregular Plural Nouns

Directions Write sentences using the plural forms of the nouns.

1. child, tooth

_____

2. woman, leaf

_____

3. sheep, deer

_____

4. goose, mouse

_____

5. man, foot

_____

Directions Write about a problem you might have in a forest. Use at least two irregular plural nouns.

_____

_____

_____

_____

Home Activity Your child learned how to use irregular plural nouns in writing. Have your child write a letter or e-mail to a family member about animals he or she has seen. Have your child use at least two irregular plural nouns in the letter or e-mail.

© Pearson Education, Inc.3

Irregular Plural Nouns

Directions Mark the letter of the plural form of each underlined noun.

1. All the <u>child</u> collect something different.
   A childs
   B childes
   C children
   D child

2. Carlo has 20 <u>foot</u> of string.
   A foots
   B feet
   C foot
   D footes

3. Jo has 8 stuffed <u>mouse</u>.
   A mouses
   B meese
   C mouse
   D mice

4. Nick has all his baby <u>tooth</u>.
   A teeth
   B teeths
   C tooth
   D tooths

5. Jake has 100 toy army <u>man</u>.
   A mans
   B man
   C men
   D manes

6. Maria has 20 plastic <u>sheep</u>.
   A sheep
   B sheeps
   C sheepes
   D sheepe

7. Nan has 15 pictures of fall <u>leaf</u>.
   A leafs
   B leavs
   C leaves
   D leafes

8. Charlie collects toy <u>deer</u>.
   A deere
   B deer
   C deers
   D deeres

Home Activity Your child prepared for taking tests on irregular plural nouns. Have a discussion with your child about the families in your neighborhood. Ask your child to use the singular and plural forms of *man, woman,* and *child.*

Irregular Plural Nouns

Directions Underline the singular nouns and circle the plural nouns in the sentences.

1. Neighbors thought the dirty park was a problem.

2. Men cut branches and raked leaves.

3. The children picked up papers.

4. The workers saw several deer and geese during the day.

5. Their feet were muddy, but the park was clean.

Directions Write the plural form of the noun in ( ).

6. A big problem was solved by those (woman). _____

7. The family's garage was full of (mouse). _____

8. The ladies brought in cats and (child). _____

9. Soon the mice ran for their (life). _____

Directions Write one or two sentences about a clean-up problem and how it was solved. Use the plural forms of at least two of these nouns: *child, foot, leaf, man.*

10. _____

_____

Home Activity Your child reviewed irregular plural nouns. Look at a newspaper article with your child. Have your child point out three irregular plural nouns.

© Pearson Education, Inc.3

Name _____

Singular Possessive Nouns

To show that one person, animal, or thing owns something, use a **singular possessive noun.** Add an apostrophe (') and the letter *s* to a singular noun to make it possessive.

Singular Noun   The <u>hare</u> planted corn.
Singular Possessive Noun   The bear wanted the <u>hare's</u> corn.

Directions Write the possessive noun in each sentence.

1. Aesop's fables tell stories about people and animals. _____

2. A fox takes a crow's cheese. _____

3. A mouse frees a lion's paw. _____

4. A wolf wears a sheep's fur. _____

5. People enjoy each story's lesson. _____

Directions Write the possessive form of the underlined noun in each sentence.

6. <u>Jeff</u> favorite fable is about the wind and the sun. _____

7. The wind challenges the <u>sun</u> power. _____

8. Which one can remove a <u>man</u> coat? _____

9. The man feels the <u>wind</u> chill, and he buttons his coat. _____

10. He pulls up his <u>coat</u> collar. _____

11. The <u>sun</u> heat makes the man warm, and he takes off his coat. _____

12. What do you think is the <u>fable</u> lesson? _____

School-Home CONNECTION

Home Activity Your child learned about singular possessive nouns. Have your child name objects in your home and use a possessive phrase to tell who they belong to, for example, *Dad's book*.

Grammar and Writing Practice Book   Unit 2 Week 4 **33**

Singular Possessive Nouns

Directions Write sentences about animal stories you know. Use the singular possessive form of each noun shown.

1. animal

_____

2. forest

_____

3. wolf

_____

4. lion

_____

5. pig

_____

Directions Write two sentences about animal characters. Use at least two singular possessive nouns.

_____

_____

_____

_____

© Pearson Education, Inc.3

Home Activity Your child learned how to use singular possessive nouns in writing. Read a story with your child. Have your child write a sentence about the story using at least one singular possessive noun.

Grammar and Writing Practice Book

Singular Possessive Nouns

Directions Mark the letter of the correct possessive noun to complete each sentence.

1. The _____ field needs water.
   A farmer
   B farmers
   C farmer's
   D farmers's

2. The _____ sunlight helps the crops.
   A day
   B day's
   C days
   D days's

3. The _____ family will help out.
   A man's
   B mans
   C mens
   D mans'

4. The _____ soil looks rich.
   A cornfields
   B cornfield's
   C cornfields's
   D cornfield

5. The _____ leaves seem healthy.
   A lettuce's
   B lettuces
   C lettuces's
   D lettuce'

6. These tomatoes grow in a big _____ shade.
   A tree
   B trees's
   C trees
   D tree's

7. The carrots grow near the _____ farm.
   A neighbor
   B neighbors
   C neighbor's
   D neighbors's

8. There will be many crops in this _____ harvest.
   A falls
   B fall's
   C falls's
   D fall'

9. The family will sell them at the _____ market.
   A town's
   B towns
   C towns's
   D town'

10. Then they will plan next _____ crops.
    A year
    B years
    C year's
    D year'

Home Activity Your child prepared for taking tests on singular possessive nouns. Have your child think of a friend's name and something that friend owns and make up a sentence using the possessive form of the friend's name.

Singular Possessive Nouns

Directions Write the correct possessive noun in ( ) to complete each sentence.

1. Rob played a trick on his (friends, friend's) brother. _____

2. He put his jacket on (Daves, Dave's) chair. _____

3. It looked just like the older (boy's, boys's) jacket. _____

4. The (jackets, jacket's) sleeves were too short for Dave. _____

5. Dave couldn't believe his (bodys, body's) amazing growth. _____

Directions Write each sentence. Use the singular possessive form of the underlined noun.

6. Tom put a toy mouse in his <u>sister</u> room.

_____

7. His parents heard <u>Annie</u> shouts.

_____

8. <u>Tom</u> parents didn't like his tricks.

_____

9. His next trick would cost a <u>week</u> allowance.

_____

Directions Should people play tricks on others? Answer in a complete sentence. Use at least one singular possessive noun.

10. _____

_____

Home Activity Your child reviewed singular possessive nouns. Say the name of a family member. Have your child write a sentence using the singular possessive form of the name.

© Pearson Education, Inc. 3

Name _____

Plural Possessive Nouns

> To show that two or more people share or own something, use a **plural possessive noun.**
>
> | | |
> |---|---|
> | **Plural Noun** | The birds built nests. |
> | **Singular Possessive Noun** | One bird's nest was made of twigs. |
> | **Plural Possessive Noun** | Some birds' nests are made of grass. |
>
> Add an apostrophe (') to plural nouns that end in *-s, -es,* or *-ies* to make them possessive. To make plural nouns that do not end in *-s, -es,* or *-ies* possessive, add an apostrophe and an *s.*
>
> children   children's toys   women   women's books

Directions Write the plural possessive noun in each sentence.

1. Eagles' nests are huge. _____

2. Hummingbirds' nests hold their eggs. _____

3. The parents' job is to protect their chicks. _____

4. The trees' holes were made by woodpeckers. _____

5. The forest's trees are full of animals' homes. _____

Directions Write the possessive form of the underlined plural noun in each sentence.

6. There are good places for our cities birds to nest. _____

7. Some pigeons homes are on window ledges. _____

8. Sometimes they get in people way. _____

9. Their babies lives can be full of danger. _____

10. Some animals destroy the bird families homes. _____

Home Activity Your child learned about plural possessive nouns. Name some families in your neighborhood. Have your child make up sentences using the plural possessive form of each noun, such as *The Smiths' dog likes to play ball.*

© Pearson Education, Inc.3

Plural Possessive Nouns

Directions Write sentences about birds and their nests. Use the plural possessive form of each noun in your sentence.

1. nests

_____

2. woodpeckers

_____

3. chicks

_____

4. weaver birds

_____

5. children

_____

Directions Write a sentence about something you like about birds and bird nests. Then write about something you do not like about them. Use at least one plural possessive noun in each sentence.

6. _____

_____

7. _____

_____

Home Activity Your child learned how to use plural possessive nouns in writing. After watching a movie or TV program, have your child write a sentence about the show that uses at least one plural possessive noun.

Plural Possessive Nouns

Directions Mark the letter of the correct singular or plural possessive noun to complete each sentence.

1. _____ homes are all different.
   A People'
   B People's
   C Peoples
   D Peoples's

2. _____ nests are very different too.
   A Birds's
   B Bird's
   C Birds'
   D Birds

3. Birds get their _____ materials from the forest.
   A home'
   B homes
   C homes's
   D homes'

4. The _____ eggs will soon hatch.
   A mothers
   B mothers's
   C mother'
   D mother's

5. The _____ hole serves as a home.
   A woodpeckers
   B woodpeckers'
   C woodpecker's
   D woodpeckers's

6. Some _____ insides are lined with feathers.
   A nest's
   B nests'
   C nest'
   D nests's

7. Most _____ nests are small.
   A hummingbirds's
   B hummingbird'
   C hummingbirds
   D hummingbirds'

8. That _____ top is a home for eagles.
   A mountains'
   B mountain's
   C mountains
   D mountain'

9. Does a _____ nest make good soup?
   A swiftlet's
   B swiftlets'
   C swiftlets
   D swiftletses'

10. The _____ taste must be unusual.
    A soups
    B soups'
    C soup's
    D soups's

Home Activity Your child prepared for taking tests on plural possessive nouns. Name some kinds of animals. Have your child write sentences using the plural possessive form of each animal name, such as *Zebras' stripes are black and white.*

Grammar and Writing Practice Book

Unit 2 Week 5 **39**

Plural Possessive Nouns

Directions Write the correct possessive noun in ( ) to complete each sentence.

1. The (children', children's) hobby is watching birds.

_____

2. They use their (parent's, parents') field glasses.

_____

3. They saw some (owl's, owls') nests.

_____

4. They heard the (animals, animals') sounds at night.

_____

Directions Write the possessive form of the underlined plural noun in each sentence.

5. The <u>chicks</u> cries were high and soft.

_____

6. The <u>babies</u> parents protected them.

_____

7. The <u>trees</u> limbs were a good home for the bird family.

_____

Directions How is your home like a bird's home? Write a sentence to answer. Use at least one plural possessive noun.

8. _____

_____

Home Activity Your child reviewed plural possessive nouns. Name three things you and your child saw or bought on a recent shopping trip. Have your child spell the plural possessive form of each item name.

Grammar and Writing Practice Book

Name _____

Action and Linking Verbs

A **verb** is a word that tells what someone or something is or does. **Action verbs** are words that show action. **Linking verbs,** such as *am, is, are, was,* and *were,* do not show action. They link a subject to a word or words in the predicate.

Action Verb	We <u>plant</u> flowers in the garden.
Linking Verb	The flowers <u>are</u> tulips.

Directions One of the underlined words in each sentence is a verb. Write that word.

1. Amy <u>puts</u> the <u>seed</u> in the ground. _____

2. She <u>covers</u> it with <u>dirt</u>. _____

3. <u>It</u> <u>is</u> a pumpkin seed. _____

4. Pumpkins <u>grow</u> in <u>summer</u>. _____

5. They <u>are</u> good <u>for</u> decorations. _____

Directions Write the sentences. Underline the verb in each sentence.

6. Ms. Alvarez grows flowers in a field.

_____

7. She sells them at a big market.

_____

8. People buy flowers for birthdays and holidays.

_____

9. Flowers are bright and cheerful.

_____

10. A bunch of flowers is a popular gift.

_____

Home Activity Your child learned about action verbs and linking verbs. Have your child name some action verbs that describe what he or she did outdoors today.

Action and Linking Verbs

Directions Add a verb to complete each sentence. Write the sentence.

1. Sam's friends _____ in the garden.

_____

2. They _____ seeds on the ground.

_____

3. Jamie _____ the rosebushes.

_____

4. The rose petals _____ as soft as velvet.

_____

5. Lucy and Lee _____ a beautiful decoration.

_____

6. They _____ the flowers on the table.

_____

Directions Write two sentences about a garden. Use one action verb and one linking verb.

_____

_____

_____

_____

Home Activity Your child learned how to use action verbs and linking verbs in writing. Have your child write a note to you about something that happened at school today. Have him or her circle each action verb and linking verb.

Name _____

Action and Linking Verbs

Directions Mark the letter of the word that is a verb.

1. It rains often in April.
  A often
  B in
  C rains
  D April

2. Flowers and trees need much water.
  A much
  B water
  C trees
  D need

3. The sun shines every day in June.
  A sun
  B shines
  C in
  D every

4. The plants are green and healthy.
  A plants
  B green
  C and
  D are

5. Plants grow tall in this season.
  A tall
  B this
  C grow
  D season

6. Josh mows the grass each week.
  A mows
  B week
  C each
  D grass

7. The weeds on the lawn are brown.
  A weeds
  B on
  C lawn
  D are

8. Sharon pulls all the weeds.
  A all
  B weeds
  C pulls
  D the

9. Animals and insects like the garden.
  A garden
  B insects
  C like
  D the

10. Ants play among the flowers all day.
  A play
  B day
  C all
  D flowers

Home Activity Your child prepared for taking tests on action verbs and linking verbs. Have your child make up some sentences about a job that interests him or her. Have your child identify the verb in each sentence.

Grammar and Writing Practice Book   Unit 3 Week 1 **43**

© Pearson Education, Inc. 3

Name _____

Action and Linking Verbs

Directions Underline the verb in each sentence. Write *A* if the verb is an action verb. Write *L* if the verb is a linking verb.

1. Tina wrote a letter to her grandma. _____

2. She told her about her visit with Aunt Maria. _____

3. The visit was short but fun. _____

4. Tina and her aunt took a picnic to the garden. _____

5. The trees in the garden were big and shady. _____

Directions Write the verb in each sentence. Write *A* after each action verb. Write *L* after each linking verb.

6. I am at the museum with Aunt Maria.

_____

7. The paintings are unusual.

_____

8. We ate lunch at a little café.

_____

9. We rode the bus all over the city.

_____

10. I was tired but happy.

_____

Home Activity Your child reviewed action verbs and linking verbs. Discuss an enjoyable outing your family has had. Have your child write one action verb and one linking verb used in the conversation.

Grammar and Writing Practice Book

Main Verbs and Helping Verbs

A **verb phrase** is a verb that has more than one word. The **main verb** shows action. A **helping verb** shows the time of the action. In the following sentence, *planting* is the main verb, and *are* is the helping verb.

   The girls are planting corn with the women.

The helping verbs *am, is,* and *are* show present time. *Was* and *were* show past time. *Will* shows future time. The helping verbs *has, have,* and *had* show that an action happened in the past. In the following sentences, *had* and *will* are helping verbs.

   They had planted in spring. We will harvest in fall.

Directions Underline the verb phrase in each sentence.

1. The chief is carving a beautiful pole.

2. He will place it at the entrance of the village.

3. The little boys are learning from the chief.

4. Someday they will carve a pole.

5. They have made many small animals already.

Directions Look at the underlined verb in each sentence. Write *M* if it is a main verb. Write *H* if it is a helping verb.

6. Everyone in the village is <u>helping</u> with the crops. _____

7. The women <u>had</u> planted the seeds. _____

8. The girls have <u>watered</u> the plants. _____

9. The boys <u>are</u> picking the beans. _____

10. The men <u>will</u> plow the fields. _____

Home Activity Your child learned about main verbs and helping verbs. Have your child answer the following question: *What were you doing at 3:00 today?* Then have your child identify the main verb and the helping verb in the answer.

Main Verbs and Helping Verbs

Directions Answer each question. Write a sentence with a main verb and a helping verb.

1. What have people made from wood?

_____

2. What kinds of trees are growing in your neighborhood?

_____

3. Suppose you are a Native American living in the Northwest many years ago. What will you do with a canoe?

_____

4. What animals familiar to the Snohomish people have you seen?

_____

5. What part of Native American life has interested you the most?

_____

Directions Write two sentences about Native American life. Use a main verb and a helping verb in each sentence.

_____

_____

_____

_____

Home Activity Your child learned how to use main verbs and helping verbs in writing. Ask your child to write a note about something he or she is looking forward to doing in the future. Have your child circle each main verb and underline each helping verb.

© Pearson Education, Inc. 3

Main Verbs and Helping Verbs

Directions Mark the letter that shows the main verb in each sentence.

1. Big trees have grown there for ages.
A have
B have grown
C grown
D grown there

2. The people have used wood for many things.
A used
B have
C people have
D have used

3. They are cutting down a fir tree.
A are cutting
B They are
C are
D cutting

4. They will build a house with it.
A They will
B build
C build a house
D will build

5. The young men had made canoes of pine.
A made
B had
C had made
D made canoes

Directions Mark the letter that shows the helping verb in each sentence.

6. I am carving a redwood bowl.
A carving
B am
C I am
D am carving

7. The new bowl will look beautiful.
A will
B will look
C look
D look beautiful

8. A boy is making a bow and arrows.
A is
B boy is
C is making
D making

9. He will use them in the forest.
A will use
B use them
C use
D will

10. We have planted more trees.
A have planted
B planted
C have
D We have

Home Activity Your child prepared for taking tests on main verbs and helping verbs. Have your child make up two sentences about what he or she will do next weekend. Ask your child to identify the main verb and the helping verb in each sentence.

Main Verbs and Helping Verbs

Directions Write the main verb and the helping verb in each sentence.

1. The women are sewing animal furs together.

Main verb: _____

Helping verb: _____

2. She is making a coat.

Main verb: _____

Helping verb: _____

3. It will keep someone warm in winter.

Main verb: _____

Helping verb: _____

4. She has created a beautiful hat from bird feathers.

Main verb: _____

Helping verb: _____

Directions Look at the underlined verb in each sentence. Write *M* if it is a main verb. Write *H* if it is a helping verb.

5. The people <u>were</u> celebrating all day. _____

6. They <u>will</u> sing and dance. _____

7. The chief had <u>planned</u> the party. _____

8. The children <u>are</u> playing games. _____

Directions Write a sentence about a celebration. Use a main verb and a helping verb. Underline the main verb. Circle the helping verb.

_____

_____

Home Activity Your child reviewed main verbs and helping verbs. Ask your child to make up a sentence about a party he or she has attended. Have your child include a main verb and a helping verb in the sentence and identify each.

Subject-Verb Agreement

The subject and the verb in a sentence must work together, or **agree.** To make most present tense verbs agree with singular nouns or *he, she,* or *it,* add *-s.* If the subject is a plural noun or *I, you, we,* or *they,* the present tense verb does not end in *-s.*

Singular Subject   The sun shines. It warms the Earth.
Plural Subject   Stars glow at night. They sparkle.

A form of *be* in a sentence also must agree with the subject. Use *is* or *was* to agree with singular nouns. Use *are* or *were* to agree with plural nouns.

Singular Subject   A star is shining. It was millions of miles away.
Plural Subject   People are gazing at stars. They were interested in them.

Directions Choose the verb in ( ) that agrees with the subject. Write the verb.

1. I (see, sees) yellow stars. _____

2. Yellow stars (is, are) very hot. _____

3. Red stars (has, have) cooler temperatures. _____

4. Stars (is, are) made of hot gas. _____

5. The sun (appear, appears) very large. _____

Directions Choose the verb in ( ) that agrees with the subject. Write the sentence.

6. Earth (move, moves) around the sun.

_____

7. Our world (spin, spins) around once a day.

_____

8. We (see, sees) many stars at night.

_____

Home Activity Your child learned about subject-verb agreement. Have your child tell a sentence about something that happened in school and explain how the subject and verb agree.

Subject-Verb Agreement

Directions Use each word or phrase as the subject of a sentence. Add a verb describing an action that takes place in the present. Make sure each verb agrees with its subject.

1. The sun

_____

2. Some stars

_____

3. Our galaxy

_____

4. A telescope

_____

5. Constellations

_____

Directions Write two sentences about stars. Use verbs that describe actions in the present.

_____

_____

_____

_____

_____

Home Activity Your child learned how to use subject-verb agreement in writing. Ask your child to write sentences in the present tense about a favorite television program. Have your child circle each verb and explain why it agrees with the subject of the sentence.

© Pearson Education, Inc. 3

Subject-Verb Agreement

Directions Mark the letter of the verb that completes each sentence.

1. Kevin _____ all about stars.
   A learn
   B learning
   C learns
   D learnes

2. He _____ his dad's telescope.
   A using
   B use
   C useses
   D uses

3. Kevin's friends _____ interested in stars too.
   A is
   B be
   C are
   D being

4. They _____ to a planetarium.
   A goes
   B go
   C going
   D gone

5. The planetarium _____ programs about stars.
   A has
   B have
   C having
   D haves

6. Tammy _____ the Milky Way.
   A view
   B viewes
   C viewing
   D views

7. The Milky Way _____ our galaxy.
   A be
   B is
   C being
   D are

8. The stars _____ bright on a dark night.
   A appears
   B appearing
   C appear
   D appeares

9. You _____ that constellation.
   A find
   B finds
   C findes
   D finding

10. We _____ the moon.
    A studies
    B studying
    C studys
    D study

Home Activity Your child prepared for taking tests on subject-verb agreement. Point out a sentence in a newspaper. Have your child identify the subject and verb in the sentence and explain why they agree.

Subject-Verb Agreement

Directions Choose the verb in ( ) that agrees with the subject. Write the verb.

1. Stars (helps, help) people with directions. _____

2. Sailors (gazes, gaze) at stars. _____

3. The North Star (stays, stay) over the North Pole. _____

4. It (is, are) a guide for sailors and pilots. _____

Directions Choose the verb in ( ) that agrees with each subject. Write the sentence.

5. Sometimes planets (looks, look) like stars.

_____

6. Those (is, are) shooting stars.

_____

7. A comet (seem, seems) like a star with a tail.

_____

8. The skies (is, are) full of bright objects.

_____

Directions Write a sentence about something you like about stars. Underline the verb. Make sure it agrees with the subject of the sentence.

_____

_____

_____

© Pearson Education, Inc.3

Home Activity Your child reviewed subject-verb agreement. Say the names of some people and groups of people in your family and neighborhood. Have your child make up a sentence in the present tense about each with a verb that agrees with the subject.

Grammar and Writing Practice Book

Name _____

A Symphony of Whales

DEVELOP THE CONCEPT

Present, Past, and Future Tenses

Verbs can show when an action happens. This is called **tense.** Different verb tenses have different forms. Many present tense verbs end in *-s*. Form the past tense of many verbs by adding *-ed*. Add the helping verb *will* to a verb to make it a future tense verb.

Present Tense	A whale stays near the beach.
Past Tense	The whale jumped out of the water.
Future Tense	The other whales will jump out soon.

- When a verb ends with *e,* drop the *e* before adding *-ed: glide   glided*
- When a one-syllable verb ends with one vowel followed by one consonant, double the final consonant before adding *-ed: shop   shopped*
- When a verb ends with a consonant followed by *y,* change the *y* to *i* before adding *-ed: hurry   hurried*

Directions Tell the tense of the underlined verb in each sentence. Write *present, past,* or *future.*

1. I like the humpback whales. _____

2. You will enjoy the whales' music. _____

3. Those whales traveled from the Arctic Ocean. _____

4. They will return next year. _____

Directions Write the verb in ( ) that correctly completes each sentence.

5. Last year Sammy's class (learn, learned) about whales. _____

6. Whales cannot breathe underwater, so they (jump, jumped) out of the water for air.

_____

7. Each time a mother whale gives birth, she (stays, stayed) close to the baby for a

year. _____

8. After a year, the baby (cared, will care) for itself.

_____

Home Activity Your child learned about present, past, and future tenses. Ask your child to make up a sentence about something he or she saw on the way home from school and identify the tense of the sentence's verb.

© Pearson Education, Inc. 3

Grammar and Writing Practice Book   Unit 3 Week 4 **53**

Present, Past, and Future Tenses

Directions Choose a verb from the word bank to replace each underlined verb. Write the sentence.

> chatter   spotted   sails   sprays

1. A boat <u>moves</u> slowly out onto the ocean.

_____

_____

2. The people on the boat <u>talk</u> excitedly.

_____

_____

3. Last week the people on the boat <u>watched</u> many whales.

_____

_____

4. Suddenly, a spout of water <u>jumps</u> out of the ocean.

_____

_____

Directions Write three sentences about whales. Use present tense in one sentence, past tense in one sentence, and future tense in one sentence.

_____

_____

_____

_____

© Pearson Education, Inc. 3

Home Activity Your child learned how to use present, past, and future tenses in writing. Ask your child to write three sentences about an after-school activity using a different tense in each sentence. Have your child identify the tense of each sentence.

Present, Past, and Future Tenses

Directions Mark the letter of the verb that completes each sentence. Use the tense in ( ).

1. We ___ for whales in the ocean. (future)
   A searched
   B will search
   C search
   D searches

2. Many whales ___ in cold water. (present)
   A lived
   B will live
   C live
   D living

3. They ___ to warm water before winter. (future)
   A travel
   B traveling
   C traveled
   D will travel

4. Whales ___ in small groups. (present)
   A stay
   B stays
   C stayed
   D will stay

5. Those whales ___ a family. (past)
   A form
   B formed
   C forming
   D will form

6. They ___ for their babies. (past)
   A care
   B will care
   C cared
   D caring

7. That baby whale ___ two tons. (present)
   A weighs
   B weighed
   C will weigh
   D weighing

8. Its size ___ you. (future)
   A will amaze
   B amazed
   C amazes
   D amazing

9. In the past, people ___ whales. (past)
   A hunt
   B hunting
   C hunts
   D hunted

10. Most people ___ at whales today. (present)
    A look
    B will look
    C looking
    D looks

Home Activity Your child prepared for taking tests on present, past, and future tenses. Point out a sentence in a book you are reading together. Have your child tell whether the sentence is in present, past, or future tense.

Present, Past, and Future Tenses

Directions Tell the tense of the underlined verb in each sentence. Write *present*, *past*, or *future*.

1. A whale <u>lives</u> at the sea park. _____

2. It <u>swims</u> under the water. _____

3. The whale <u>amazed</u> its trainers. _____

4. People <u>will cheer</u> the clever whale. _____

Directions Choose a verb from the list to replace each underlined word or words. Change each verb to the correct tense if necessary. Write the sentence.

> view   leap   enjoy

5. A dolphin <u>will jump</u> out of the water.

_____

6. Ms. Kenny <u>watched</u> dolphins through the window.

_____

7. People <u>like</u> dolphins.

_____

Directions Write a sentence about an animal in a sea park. Underline the verb. Tell whether it is present, past, or future tense.

_____

_____

_____

Home Activity Your child reviewed present, past, and future tenses. Say a sentence about the community you live in. Ask your child to identify the verb and the verb tense in your sentence.

56 Unit 3 Week 4

Grammar and Writing Practice Book

Name _____

Irregular Verbs

Usually you add *-ed* to a verb to show past tense. **Irregular verbs** do not follow this rule. Instead of having *-ed* forms to show past tense, irregular verbs change to other words.

Present Tense	We <u>do</u> a report on water.
Past Tense	We <u>did</u> a report on water.
Past with *has, have,* or *had*	We <u>have done</u> reports on water.

Irregular verbs have a special form when they are used with *has, have,* and *had*. Use the special past forms in the third column of the chart only with these helping verbs.

Here are some irregular verbs and their past forms:

Present Tense	Past Tense	Past with *has, have,* or *had*
begin	began	*(has, have, had)* begun
do	did	*(has, have, had)* done
find	found	*(has, have, had)* found
give	gave	*(has, have, had)* given
go	went	*(has, have, had)* gone
run	ran	*(has, have, had)* run
see	saw	*(has, have, had)* seen
take	took	*(has, have, had)* taken
think	thought	*(has, have, had)* thought
wear	wore	*(has, have, had)* worn

Directions Choose the correct form of the irregular verb in ( ) to complete each sentence. Write the verb on the line.

1. The water (begun, began) at the top of the mountain. _____

2. The stream (go, went) down the hill. _____

3. It (run, ran) into a big river. _____

4. Many people have (taken, took) water from the river. _____

5. Some have (gave, given) water to their neighbors. _____

Home Activity Your child learned about irregular verbs. Ask your child this question: *What did you wear to school today?* Have your child answer with a sentence using *wear* in the past tense (*wore*).

Irregular Verbs

Directions Write sentences about water. Use each given word in the past tense.

1. find

_____

2. think

_____

3. run

_____

4. go

_____

5. take

_____

Directions Write three sentences describing how you used fresh water in the last day. Use the past tense of at least two irregular verbs.

_____

_____

_____

_____

_____

Home Activity Your child learned how to use irregular verbs in writing. Have your child write a sentence about something your family did on a recent weekend using an irregular verb in the sentence.

© Pearson Education, Inc. 3

Irregular Verbs

Directions Mark the letter of the verb that completes each sentence.

1. Jamie has ___ a glacier in Alaska.
   A saw
   B see
   C seen
   D seed

2. The glacier ___ as packed snow.
   A begun
   B began
   C begin
   D beginning

3. It has ___ years to form.
   A took
   B taken
   C taked
   D take

4. The glacier has ___ slowly down the hill.
   A go
   B went
   C gone
   D going

5. In spring the glacier will ___ to melt.
   A begin
   B began
   C begun
   D beginning

6. The water will ___ into the ocean.
   A runs
   B ran
   C run
   D running

7. People have ___ the glacier a name.
   A give
   B gave
   C giving
   D given

8. The glacier has ___ a path down the mountain.
   A wear
   B weared
   C wore
   D worn

9. We have ___ fresh glacier water.
   A find
   B found
   C finding
   D finded

10. Jamie ___ the glacier was amazing.
    A think
    B thinking
    C thinked
    D thought

Home Activity Your child prepared for taking tests on irregular verbs. In a magazine or newspaper, point out a verb. Have your child tell whether the verb is regular or irregular.

Irregular Verbs

Directions Write each sentence. Use the past form of the underlined verb. Each new verb will be one word.

1. We <u>take</u> care of our water supply.

_____

2. Everyone <u>thinks</u> about water.

_____

3. Some people almost <u>run</u> out of fresh water.

_____

4. Taking care of water <u>begins</u> with us.

_____

Directions Write each sentence. Use the past form of the verb in ( ) to complete each sentence.

5. We have (find, found) fresh water underground.

_____

6. The dam (gave, given) the town energy from water.

_____

7. Big pipes have (taken, took) water to the city.

_____

Directions Write a sentence about saving water. Use the past tense of an irregular verb. Underline it.

8. _____

Home Activity Your child reviewed irregular verbs. Ask your child this question: *What did I give you for your birthday?* Have your child answer in a sentence using the past tense of *give* (gave).

Grammar and Writing Practice Book

© Pearson Education, Inc. 3

Singular and Plural Pronouns

Pronouns are words that take the place of nouns. Pronouns that take the place of singular nouns are **singular pronouns**. *I, me, he, she, him, her,* and *it* are singular pronouns.

Singular Pronoun The <u>man</u> cannot fly. <u>He</u> cannot fly.

Pronouns that take the place of plural nouns are **plural pronouns**. *We, us, they,* and *them* are plural pronouns.

Plural Pronoun   <u>Penguins</u> cannot fly. <u>They</u> cannot fly.

You can be used as a singular and a plural pronoun.

<u>Orville and Wilbur</u>, why do <u>you</u> want to fly?
<u>Orville</u>, <u>you</u> will be the first to fly.

Directions Write the pronoun in each sentence.

1. People do not have wings, so we cannot fly. _____

2. Flying has always interested us. _____

3. The Wright brothers wanted to fly, so they built an airplane. _____

4. I have never flown in an airplane. _____

5. Uncle Joe is a pilot, and he flies often. _____

Directions Write *S* if the underlined pronoun is singular. Write *P* if it is plural.

6. Inventors were clever, and <u>they</u> made all kinds of flying machines. _____

7. They built wings and attached <u>them</u> to their bodies. _____

8. They made a balloon, and <u>it</u> had a big bucket for passengers. _____

9. <u>We</u> still remember Amelia Earhart. _____

10. <u>She</u> flew all over the world in the early days of airplanes. _____

Home Activity Your child learned about singular and plural pronouns. Make up sentences about one or more members of your family. Have your child repeat the sentences using pronouns in place of people's names.

Singular and Plural Pronouns

Directions Revise each sentence. Replace the underlined words with singular or plural pronouns.

1. Some people made a kite, and <u>the kite</u> lifted <u>the people</u> into the air.

_____

_____

2. An inventor made big wings, but <u>the wings</u> could not support <u>the inventor</u>.

_____

_____

3. An inventor made a glider, and <u>the glider</u> had wings that made <u>the glider</u> sail through the air.

_____

_____

4. The first airplanes did not have an engine, and <u>the airplanes</u> were heavy.

_____

_____

5. Orville Wright flew an airplane in 1903, but <u>Orville Wright</u> didn't fly <u>the airplane</u> very far.

_____

_____

Directions Write three sentences about airplanes. Use at least two different pronouns in the sentences. Underline the pronouns.

_____

_____

Home Activity Your child learned how to use singular and plural pronouns in writing. Have your child write two sentences about a current event using a singular and a plural pronoun.

Grammar and Writing Practice Book

Singular and Plural Pronouns

Directions Mark the letter of the pronoun that can replace the underlined word or words.

1. The <u>Wright brothers</u> built airplanes.
   A He
   B She
   C They
   D We

2. <u>A Frenchman</u> flew from France to England in 1909.
   A They
   B He
   C We
   D Him

3. Pilots flew <u>airplanes</u> during World War I.
   A it
   B him
   C they
   D them

4. <u>Amelia Earhart</u> crossed the Atlantic.
   A She
   B He
   C They
   D You

5. <u>Passengers</u> flew many places in 1936.
   A He
   B She
   C They
   D Us

6. Nice cabins made <u>passengers</u> comfortable.
   A him
   B it
   C her
   D them

7. <u>A flying boat</u> carried people across oceans.
   A They
   B It
   C He
   D She

8. Pilots flew <u>jets</u> in the 1950s.
   A them
   B it
   C him
   D her

9. <u>A rocket</u> went into space in 1961.
   A They
   B He
   C It
   D Them

10. <u>People</u> could really fly!
    A It
    B She
    C Him
    D We

Home Activity Your child prepared for taking tests on singular and plural pronouns. Read a book with your child. Point out several sentences with pronouns. Have your child identify the pronouns and tell whether they are singular or plural.

© Pearson Education, Inc. 3

Singular and Plural Pronouns

Directions Write *S* if the underlined pronoun is singular. Write *P* if it is plural.

1. An airplane has wings, and <u>they</u> are shaped like a bird's wings. _____

2. The wing is curved, and <u>it</u> helps a bird fly. _____

3. Flaps of the wings move <u>them</u> along. _____

4. The wing's design amazes <u>me</u>. _____

5. Students, <u>you</u> could never invent a wing like this. _____

Directions Write each sentence. Replace the underlined word or words with the correct pronoun.

6. <u>Birds</u> have many different kinds of wings.

_____

7. A <u>seagull</u> has long, pointed wings.

_____

8. Short, rounded wings help <u>hawks</u> fly.

_____

Directions Write a sentence about a bird flying. Use a pronoun. Underline it and write *S* if it is singular or *P* if it is plural.

_____

_____

_____

Home Activity Your child reviewed singular and plural pronouns. On an outdoor walk, discuss birds with your child. Have your child identify at least two pronouns used in your discussion.

© Pearson Education, Inc.3

Subject and Object Pronouns

A pronoun used as the subject of a sentence is called a **subject pronoun.** A pronoun used after an action verb or as the object of a preposition is called an **object pronoun.**

- *I, you, he, she, it, we,* and *they* are subject pronouns.
- *Me, you, him, her, it, us,* and *them* are object pronouns.

Subject Pronouns <u>They</u> visited Mount Rainier. Sam and <u>I</u> went too.

Object Pronouns The mountain amazed <u>them</u>. They took pictures of Sam and <u>me</u>.

Directions Write the pronouns in each sentence.

1. She was on a high mountain, and the wind bothered her. _____

2. In the desert, the sun beats down on you. _____

3. The Mississippi is a long river, and it has many kinds of fish. _____

4. The huge waterfall impressed him. _____

5. He and I watched the tide come into shore. _____

Directions Write *SP* if the underlined pronoun is a subject pronoun. Write *OP* if it is an object pronoun.

6. Lake Superior is the largest of the Great Lakes. <u>It</u> is also the deepest. _____

7. The lake's size interested <u>us</u>. _____

8. Jamal visited Africa. There <u>he</u> saw the Nile River. _____

9. The rains in the tropical forest drenched <u>them</u>. _____

10. The deep snow on the mountain surprised Tina and <u>him</u>. _____

Home Activity Your child learned about subject and object pronouns. Make up sentences about book and movie characters. Have your child repeat the sentences with pronouns in place of the characters' names.

© Pearson Education, Inc. 3

Subject and Object Pronouns

Directions Write each sentence. Replace the underlined words with subject or object pronouns.

1. When some people visited the South Pole, <u>the people</u> wore heavy coats to keep <u>the people</u> warm.

   _____

   _____

2. Bob hiked in the desert, and <u>Bob</u> took plenty of water with <u>Bob</u>.

   _____

   _____

3. Because the island is very wet, <u>the island</u> has many kinds of plants and animals.

   _____

   _____

4. As Jack and Chris climbed the mountain, a guide went with <u>Jack and Chris</u>.

   _____

   _____

Directions Write three sentences about a place you think is amazing. Use at least one subject pronoun and one object pronoun. Underline the pronouns.

   _____

   _____

   _____

   _____

© Pearson Education, Inc. 3

Home Activity Your child learned how to use subject and object pronouns in writing. Ask your child to write two sentences about an interesting place he or she has seen. Have your child use a subject pronoun and an object pronoun.

Grammar and Writing Practice Book

Subject and Object Pronouns

Directions Mark the letter of the pronoun that correctly replaces the underlined word or words.

1. <u>Parrots</u> live in the rain forest.
   A Them
   B She
   C Him
   D They

2. The South Pole is home to <u>penguins</u>.
   A them
   B they
   C her
   D him

3. The river delighted <u>Maria</u>.
   A it
   B she
   C her
   D them

4. <u>A climber</u> reached the peak of Mount Everest.
   A She
   B Her
   C They
   D Them

5. Cold winds blasted <u>the mountains</u>.
   A they
   B them
   C her
   D it

6. Anna and <u>Sue</u> swam in the ocean.
   A him
   B her
   C he
   D she

7. <u>The boys</u> visited the desert.
   A Them
   B Him
   C He
   D They

8. Camels carried Mark and <u>Jim</u>.
   A I
   B them
   C him
   D he

9. Antarctica is too cold for <u>you and I</u>.
   A we
   B us
   C them
   D they

10. <u>You and I</u> will like the rain forest.
    A We
    B Us
    C Them
    D They

Home Activity Your child prepared for taking tests on subject and object pronouns. Discuss a visit to a farm or zoo with your child. Have your child identify pronouns in the sentences and tell whether they are subject pronouns or object pronouns.

Subject and Object Pronouns

Directions Write *SP* if the underlined pronoun is a subject pronoun. Write *OP* if it is an object pronoun.

1. Sir Edmund Hillary was a climber. <u>He</u> reached the top of Mount Everest.

   _____

2. Tenzing Norgay, a guide, went with <u>him</u>. _____

3. Many climbers go to Everest, and the climb challenges <u>them</u>. _____

4. <u>They</u> use all their strength for the climb. _____

5. <u>You</u> could climb Mount Everest. _____

Directions Choose the correct pronoun for each sentence. Write the sentence.

6. Thomas and (me, I) went to Niagara Falls.

   _____

7. The falls amazed (we, us).

   _____

8. (Him, He) and I took pictures of the crashing water.

   _____

Directions Write a sentence about a mountain. Use a pronoun. Underline it and write *SP* if it is a subject pronoun or *OP* if it is an object pronoun.

   _____

   _____

   _____

Home Activity Your child reviewed subject and object pronouns. On a walk or drive, ask your child to find a pronoun on a sign. Have your child tell whether it is a subject pronoun or an object pronoun.

Possessive Pronouns

Some pronouns show who or what owns, or possesses, something. This kind of pronoun is a **possessive pronoun.**

Possessive Pronouns   *My, mine, your, yours, her, hers, our, ours, his, their, theirs,* and *its* are possessive pronouns.

• This is <u>my</u> gold rock, and that is <u>hers</u>.

Directions Write the possessive pronouns in each sentence.

1. When Tracy visited her granddad, she looked for rocks on his farm.

   _____

2. Her favorite rock was limestone. _____

3. Its color was pale gray. _____

4. Her brothers found rocks, and they put them in their granddad's study.

   _____

5. They had a shelf for theirs, and Tracy had a shelf for hers. _____

Directions Choose the possessive pronoun in ( ) that could replace the underlined words in each sentence. Write the sentence.

6. I found a piece of marble, and <u>the marble's</u> color was pink. (their, its)

   _____

7. Your favorite rock is quartz, and <u>my favorite rock</u> is marble. (mine, my)

   _____

8. Is this quartz <u>the quartz you own</u>? (his, yours)

   _____

Home Activity Your child learned about possessive pronouns. With your child, take turns using possessive pronouns in sentences about objects that family members collect. Have your child identify the possessive pronouns in the sentences.

© Pearson Education, Inc.3

Possessive Pronouns

Directions Revise each sentence. Replace the underlined words with possessive pronouns.

1. Daniel chose certain rocks because <u>the rocks'</u> color was bright blue.

_____

_____

2. Daniel and Matt spent all day at a creek since <u>the creek's</u> shores were covered with rocks.

_____

_____

3. Daniel and Matt looked for interesting rocks, and <u>Daniel and Matt's</u> bag was soon full.

_____

_____

4. Matt found a snowy white rock, which was <u>Matt's</u> favorite.

_____

_____

Directions Write three sentences about a collection owned by you or someone else. Use at least two possessive pronouns. Underline the possessive pronouns.

_____

_____

_____

Home Activity Your child learned how to use possessive pronouns in writing. Have your child write two sentences about his or her favorite toys. Have your child underline possessive pronouns in the sentences.

© Pearson Education, Inc. 3

Grammar and Writing Practice Book

Possessive Pronouns

Directions Mark the letter of the pronoun that correctly completes each sentence.

1. I have cool rocks in ___ collection.
   A him
   B yours
   C my
   D mine

2. My dad gave me a rock from ___ collection.
   A mine
   B theirs
   C his
   D ours

3. The rock is odd, and ___ color is orange.
   A its
   B her
   C our
   D their

4. Dad taught ___ family about rocks.
   A our
   B mine
   C hers
   D its

5. We went to a big hill for ___ first lesson.
   A yours
   B its
   C mine
   D our

6. My sister Tara got down on ___ knees.
   A mine
   B yours
   C her
   D its

7. She found quartz on ___ first try.
   A him
   B her
   C yours
   D mine

8. That is your rock, and this is ___.
   A my
   B mine
   C her
   D their

9. You will know a rock by ___ color.
   A their
   B our
   C its
   D her

10. Rock collecting is a good hobby, and it could be ___.
    A my
    B yours
    C her
    D their

Home Activity Your child prepared for taking tests on possessive pronouns. Play a board game with your child. Have your child identify possessive pronouns used by any player as you play.

© Pearson Education, Inc. 3

Possessive Pronouns

Directions Circle the correct possessive pronoun for each sentence.

1. Gems are some of (our, ours) most valuable rocks.

2. (Their, Theirs) favorite gem is bright green.

3. Diamonds are found in (my, mine) state.

4. A ruby is a beautiful gem, and (her, its) color is red.

5. Ruby is my birthstone, and diamond is (her, hers).

Directions Write the possessive pronouns in each sentence.

6. Our grandmother has some beautiful gems in her collection.

   _____

7. I love the diamond for its brilliant sparkle.

   _____

8. My brother James likes the rubies and their deep red color.

   _____

9. Grandma has a gem called a moonstone, and it is her favorite.

   _____

10. He wanted an emerald, and he received it for his birthday.

   _____

Directions Revise the sentence. Replace the underlined words with a possessive pronoun.

   I found a piece of marble, and <u>the marble's</u> color was pink.

   _____

   _____

School-Home CONNECTION **Home Activity** Your child reviewed possessive pronouns. While cleaning a room in your home, ask your child to use possessive pronouns to tell who owns various items.

Grammar and Writing Practice Book

Name _____

Contractions

A **contraction** is a word made by putting two words together. When words are joined in a contraction, an apostrophe shows where a letter or letters have been left out.

- Some contractions combine a pronoun and a verb: *I + am = I'm; he + is = he's; we + are = we're; you + will = you'll; we + will = we'll; they + are = they're.*
- Some contractions combine a verb and *not: can + not = can't; is + not = isn't; do + not = don't; will + not = won't; are + not = aren't.*

Contractions   They're swimming in the lake, but I can't see them.

Directions Write the contraction in each sentence.

1. Watch the Olympics, and you'll see some great swimmers. _____

2. The Americans think they'll win many medals. _____

3. I won't miss their big race tonight. _____

4. I can't believe she broke the world record. _____

5. Maybe we'll swim in the Olympics someday. _____

Directions Write the contraction in each sentence. Then write the words that make up the contraction.

6. They're starting the race. _____

7. Jeremy is in this race, and he's in the first lane. _____

8. It's important to get a fast start. _____

9. Isn't a fast turn important also? _____

10. The other swimmers can't beat Jeremy. _____

Home Activity Your child learned about contractions. With your child, read an article in a local newspaper. Have your child identify the contractions and the words that make up each contraction.

Contractions

Directions Write each sentence. Replace the underlined words with contractions.

1. <u>I am</u> studying the history of swimming.

_____

_____

2. I learned about a popular stroke of the 1800s, and <u>it is</u> called the Australian crawl.

_____

_____

3. Johnny Weismuller, an American swimmer, <u>was not</u> happy with the Australian crawl.

_____

_____

4. <u>He is</u> known for inventing the front crawl.

_____

_____

5. Now <u>we are</u> all using the front crawl.

_____

_____

Directions Write three sentences about swimming. Use at least two contractions. Underline the contractions.

_____

_____

_____

Home Activity Your child learned how to use contractions in writing. Have your child write two sentences with contractions about water activities he or she enjoys. Have your child point out the contractions.

Grammar and Writing Practice Book

Contractions

Directions Mark the letter of the correct contraction for the underlined words.

1. Swimming <u>is not</u> difficult.
   A isnt
   B it's
   C isn't
   D is'nt

2. <u>You will</u> learn some strokes.
   A You're
   B You'll
   C You'd
   D Your

3. <u>They are</u> your arm movements.
   A They're
   B They'd
   C They'll
   D Their

4. <u>I will</u> show you a kick.
   A I'd
   B I'm
   C Ill
   D I'll

5. <u>It is</u> the most popular kick.
   A Its
   B It's
   C It'd
   D It'll

6. <u>Do not</u> forget to breathe right.
   A Dont
   B Do'nt
   C Don't
   D Doesnt

7. Breathing <u>will not</u> be hard for you.
   A wasn't
   B weren't
   C won't
   D we'll

8. Races <u>are not</u> hard either.
   A isn't
   B are'nt
   C arent
   D aren't

9. <u>We are</u> learning the basic strokes first.
   A We're
   B We'll
   C We'd
   D Were

10. Then <u>we will</u> swim in races.
    A we're
    B won't
    C we'd
    D we'll

Home Activity Your child prepared for taking tests on contractions. Together sort through the mail and have your child find contractions in advertisements and notices.

Contractions

Directions Write the contraction in each sentence. Then write the words that make up the contraction.

1. I learned a new swimming stroke, and it's called the butterfly.

   _____

2. Some Olympic swimmers do the butterfly, and they're really fast.

   _____

3. Michael Phelps does the butterfly, and he's one of the world's fastest swimmers.

   _____

4. I'm learning to do the butterfly gracefully. _____

5. I think you'll enjoy the butterfly too. _____

Directions Write the sentences. Replace the underlined words with a contraction.

6. I learned the breaststroke, and it <u>was not</u> easy.

   _____

7. I <u>could not</u> move my arms and legs correctly.

   _____

8. My friend Rosa learned the breaststroke, and <u>she is</u> good at it.

   _____

9. I <u>did not</u> get too far with this new stroke.

   _____

10. From now on <u>I will</u> stick with the backstroke!

    _____

Home Activity Your child reviewed contractions. Ask your child to answer the following questions using complete sentences with contractions: *Will you go swimming next summer? Would you like to be in the Olympics?*

Name _____

Prepositions

A **preposition** is the first word in a group of words called a prepositional phrase. A **prepositional phrase** ends with a noun or pronoun called the **object of the preposition.** A prepositional phrase tells more about other words in a sentence.

Preposition	The eagle flew <u>in</u> a circle.
Prepositional Phrase	The eagle flew <u>in a circle</u>.
Object of Preposition	The eagle flew in a <u>circle</u>.

Common Prepositions

Here are some prepositions: *about, above, across, after, against, along, among, around, at, before, behind, below, beneath, beside, between, beyond, by, down, during, except, for, from, in, inside, into, near, of, off, on, onto, out, outside, over, past, since, through, throughout, to, toward, under, underneath, until, up, upon, with, within, without.*

Directions Write the preposition in each sentence.

1. Our class read a book about eagles. _____

2. Bald eagles live in the United States. _____

3. Bald eagles can grab fish from the water. _____

4. The bald eagle population decreased during the 1970s. _____

Directions Write the prepositional phrase in each sentence. Underline the preposition.

5. Another eagle within the United States is the golden eagle.

_____

6. Golden eagles have golden brown feathers on their necks.

_____

Home Activity Your child learned about prepositions. With your child, look at ads. Have your child identify five prepositional phrases.

Grammar and Writing Practice Book

© Pearson Education, Inc.3

Prepositions

Directions Add a prepositional phrase to each sentence to make it more specific. Use a prepositional phrase from the box or a prepositional phrase of your own.

through the air	on their tails	in the lake
at the national park	at the library	on high cliffs

1. We saw eagles.

_____

2. The eagles had white feathers.

_____

3. They glided.

_____

4. The eagles built nests.

_____

5. The eagles hunted fish.

_____

6. We will study eagles.

_____

Directions Write two sentences about seeing wildlife. Use at least two prepositional phrases. Underline the prepositional phrases.

_____

_____

_____

Home Activity Your child learned how to use prepositions in writing. Have your child write a sentence about a bird that includes a prepositional phrase. Ask your child to point to the prepositional phrase, the preposition, and the object of the preposition.

Grammar and Writing Practice Book

Prepositions

Directions Mark the letter of the word in each sentence that is a preposition.

1. Eagles live throughout the world.
   A the
   B throughout
   C world
   D live

2. They build their nests on treetops.
   A build
   B their
   C nests
   D on

3. The eagles fly around the lake.
   A around
   B the
   C lake
   D fly

4. Eagles eagerly swoop for prey.
   A swoop
   B for
   C prey
   D eagerly

5. They spot prey from the air.
   A spot
   B the
   C from
   D air

6. They have wings of an unusual size.
   A an
   B of
   C have
   D wings

7. They dive quickly to the ground.
   A dive
   B ground
   C the
   D to

8. Eagles hunt during the day.
   A during
   B hunt
   C day
   D the

9. They rest at night.
   A they
   B rest
   C at
   D night

10. Facts about eagles interest me.
    A interest
    B me
    C about
    D eagles

Home Activity Your child prepared for taking tests on prepositions. Look through a cookbook with your child. Ask him or her to find three prepositional phrases in a recipe and identify the preposition in each one.

Prepositions

Directions Write the prepositional phrase in each sentence. Underline the preposition.

1. A chicken has a comb on its head.

_____

2. The comb is located above the beak.

_____

3. Each type of chicken has a different comb.

_____

4. The one with the zigzag comb is a White Leghorn rooster.

_____

Directions Choose the preposition in ( ) that makes sense in each sentence. Write the sentence.

5. Chickens and eagles are different ___ one another. (above, from)

_____

6. Chickens fly only ___ short distances. (for, below)

_____

7. Eagles can soar high ___ the sky. (off, in)

_____

8. Chickens often live ___ farms. (on, out)

_____

Home Activity Your child reviewed prepositions. Ask your child to use sentences with prepositional phrases to answer these questions: *Where do you do your homework? When do you do your homework?*

Name _____

Adjectives and Articles

An **adjective** is a word that describes a person, place, or thing. Adjectives tell more about nouns. *A, an,* and *the* are special kinds of adjectives called **articles.**

> Adjectives   <u>Some</u> girls wore <u>long</u>, <u>bright</u> skirts.
> Articles   <u>A</u> boy wore <u>an</u> awesome shirt to <u>the</u> party.

- The articles *a* and *an* are used only with singular nouns. *A* is used before a word that begins with a consonant sound: *a jacket, a full cup. An* is used before a word that begins with a vowel sound: *an eagle, an orange jacket, an empty cup.*
- Use *the* before singular or plural nouns: *the shoe, the shoes.*

Directions Write the adjective that describes each underlined noun.

1. Many countries have colorful <u>clothing</u> for celebrations. _____

2. Indian women wear silk <u>dresses</u>. _____

3. Many Scottish men have plaid <u>kilts</u> for special occasions. _____

4. In Russia, men put on long <u>coats</u>. _____

5. Japanese kimonos are made in many <u>colors</u>. _____

Directions Circle the article in ( ) that correctly completes each sentence.

6. The American Indian wore (a, an) jacket with colorful beads.

7. (A, The) short pants that man is wearing are German.

8. The African man wore (a, an) orange robe.

9. (The, A) Mexican musicians had big hats.

10. The woman from Chile wore (a, an) outfit with a long, white skirt.

Home Activity Your child learned about adjectives and articles. On a walk, ask your child to use adjectives to describe various objects, such as a house, a tree, and a dog.

Name _____

Suki's Kimono

APPLY TO WRITING

Adjectives and Articles

Directions Complete each sentence by adding an adjective. Write the new sentence.

1. Everyone wore ___ clothes to the party.

_____

_____

2. Amy had on her ___ blouse.

_____

_____

3. The ___ shirt is Kevin's.

_____

_____

4. Julio and William came with ___ hats on their heads.

_____

_____

5. Kay's ___ pants made us laugh.

_____

_____

Directions Write two sentences about your favorite outfit. Use at least two adjectives. Underline the adjectives.

_____

_____

_____

Home Activity Your child learned how to use adjectives and articles in writing. Ask your child to write a sentence about a costume he or she has worn. Have your child use one or more adjectives in the sentence and identify them.

© Pearson Education, Inc. 3

Grammar and Writing Practice Book

Adjectives and Articles

Directions Mark the letter of the word that is an adjective.

1. Tim wore his black shoes.
   A wore
   B shoes
   C Tim
   D black

2. I wore old sneakers.
   A I
   B wore
   C old
   D sneakers

3. I wear cool sandals in summer.
   A in
   B cool
   C wear
   D summer

4. Bill wears warm boots in winter.
   A warm
   B wears
   C boots
   D winter

5. Kyle found an orange sock.
   A found
   B orange
   C sock
   D Kyle

6. Ann's shoes have thin straps.
   A thin
   B straps
   C have
   D shoes

7. Do you need more shoes?
   A shoes
   B you
   C need
   D more

8. I can run in my new shoes.
   A can
   B run
   C in
   D new

9. The Dutch girl wore wooden shoes.
   A girl
   B shoes
   C wooden
   D wore

10. The Swiss girl wore shiny boots.
    A shiny
    B wore
    C boots
    D girl

© Pearson Education, Inc. 3

Home Activity Your child prepared for taking tests on adjectives and articles. Circle a paragraph in a newspaper or magazine article. Ask your child to count the articles in the paragraph.

Name _____

Adjectives and Articles

Directions Circle each article. Underline each adjective.

1. People have worn many different styles throughout the years.

2. When Aunt Rose was a teacher, she wore long, straight skirts.

3. Grandma wore nice dresses to school.

4. My mom often wore old jeans in the classroom.

5. A popular style in some schools today is a uniform.

Directions Circle the article in ( ) that correctly completes each sentence.

6. People wear different clothes all over (an, the) world.

7. No one needs (a, an) heavy coat in Hawaii.

8. (A, An) overcoat is needed in Russia.

9. You can wear (a, an) shirt with short sleeves all year in Costa Rica.

10. (A, An) extra raincoat comes in handy in England.

Directions Write two sentences describing the clothes you are wearing today. Use at least two adjectives in each sentence. Circle each article and underline each adjective in your sentences.

_____

_____

_____

_____

Home Activity Your child reviewed adjectives and articles. Discuss the day's weather with your child. Ask him or her to identify some adjectives used in the conversation.

84 Unit 5 Week 1

Grammar and Writing Practice Book

© Pearson Education, Inc. 3

Adjectives That Compare

Adjectives are often used to make comparisons. To compare two people, places, or things, you usually add *-er* to an adjective to make a comparative adjective. To compare three or more people, places, or things, you usually add *-est* to an adjective to make a superlative adjective.

Sometimes you must change the spelling of an adjective when you write the *-er* or *-est* form.

Drop final *e*	fine	finer	finest
Change *y* to *i*	easy	easier	easiest
Double final consonant	big	bigger	biggest

Chicago is a <u>bigger</u> city than Baltimore.
New York is the <u>biggest</u> city in the United States.

Directions Underline the adjective that compares in each sentence.

1. Abuelito goes to the seashore on the sunniest day of the week.

2. This fish is smaller than that one.

3. Abuelito makes the prettiest kite of all.

4. Abuelito has the cleanest aquarium in town.

5. Some fish in the aquarium are bigger than others.

Directions Write *C* if the underlined adjective is a comparative adjective. Write *S* if it is a superlative adjective.

6. Grandpa had a <u>harder</u> childhood than his granddaughter. _____

7. Grandma's grandmother had the <u>longest</u> trip to California. _____

8. The <u>roughest</u> ride was in a covered wagon. _____

9. Was Grandpa's trip from Europe <u>easier</u>? _____

10. Abuelita is the <u>proudest</u> grandparent. _____

Home Activity Your child learned about adjectives that compare. Ask your child to describe some television programs using adjectives that compare.

© Pearson Education, Inc. 3

Adjectives That Compare

Directions Add a comparative or superlative adjective to complete each sentence. Use a form of an adjective from the box or an adjective of your own. Make any necessary spelling changes. Write the new sentence.

tasty	nice	bright	cute	large

1. The kite was the _____ kite in the sky.

_____

2. Abuelita's *huevos rancheros* is the _____ breakfast of all.

_____

_____

3. The circus elephant is _____ than the tiger.

_____

4. The colorful balloons were the _____ surprise in the world.

_____

_____

5. Is Grandma's tabby cat _____ than Abuelita's dog?

_____

Directions Write two sentences comparing two or more pets or other animals. Use at least two adjectives that compare. Underline the adjectives.

_____

_____

_____

Home Activity Your child learned how to use adjectives that compare in writing. Have your child write a note to a friend or family member that includes one or more adjectives that compare.

Adjectives That Compare

Directions Mark the letter of the adjective that correctly completes each sentence.

1. Her grandparents are ___ about her visit.
   A happiest
   B happy
   C more happy
   D most happy

2. Grandma's breakfast is ___ than Abuelita's breakfast.
   A big
   B more big
   C bigger
   D biggest

3. Pancakes with honey are ___ than eggs.
   A sweeter
   B sweetest
   C sweet
   D most sweet

4. The circus is ___ than a day at the beach.
   A lively
   B liveliest
   C most lively
   D livelier

5. A piñata is the ___ part of the party.
   A great
   B greater
   C greatest
   D more great

6. A new doll was the ___ birthday present of all.
   A prettiest
   B pretty
   C more pretty
   D prettier

7. This aquarium fish is ___ than that one.
   A new
   B most new
   C newest
   D newer

8. Grandma has a ___ owl collection.
   A large
   B larger
   C largest
   D more large

9. The kite is ___ than the balloons.
   A highest
   B most high
   C higher
   D high

10. Her grandparents are the ___ grandparents in the world.
    A more nice
    B nicer
    C nice
    D nicest

Home Activity Your child prepared for taking tests on adjectives that compare. Have your child find two adjectives that compare in a letter or an e-mail from a friend or family member.

Adjectives That Compare

Directions Underline the adjective that compares in each sentence.

1. My grandma's house is closer than your grandma's house.

2. My grandpa is older than my grandma.

3. Dan's grandpa is the youngest grandpa of all.

4. I play the trickiest card game with my grandma.

5. Ana's grandpa is smarter than anyone.

Directions Choose the adjective in ( ) that correctly completes each sentence. Write the adjective on the line.

6. Her grandparents have (stranger, strangest) hobbies than mine do.

   _____

7. Grandpa had the (healthier, healthiest) year ever.

   _____

8. Those old pictures of Grandma are the (cuter, cutest) of all.

   _____

9. Grandma wore (fancier, fanciest) hats back then.

   _____

10. Grandpa had a (happier, happiest) birthday this year than last year.

    _____

11. Grandpa tells the (funnier, funniest) jokes in the world.

    _____

12. My grandparents give the (finer, finest) gifts of all.

    _____

Home Activity Your child reviewed adjectives that compare. While listening to music with your child, discuss what you like and dislike. Have your child name some adjectives that compare used in the discussion.

© Pearson Education, Inc. 3

Grammar and Writing Practice Book

Adverbs

An **adverb** is a word that can tell when, where, or how something happens.

Now the movers pack the furniture. (when)
They carry the furniture <u>outside</u>. (where)
They <u>carefully</u> load the van. (how)

- Adverbs can come before or after the verbs they describe.
- Adverbs that tell how something happens often end in *-ly*.

Directions Underline the adverbs in the sentences.

1. Kim's mother often cooks Korean dishes.

2. She chops cabbage carefully.

3. She gently mixes more vegetables.

4. She quickly cooks the mixture on the stove.

Directions Choose the correct word in ( ) to write each new sentence.

5. Everyone (usual, usually) wears costumes to the school party.

_____

_____

6. Kim (happily, happy) wears her Korean outfit.

_____

7. The jacket fits (tight, tightly) around her shoulders.

_____

8. The skirt falls (loosely, loose) around her feet.

_____

© Pearson Education, Inc. 3

Home Activity Your child learned about adverbs. Ask your child to describe something he or she did today using one or more adverbs.

Adverbs

Directions Make each sentence more specific by adding an adverb from the box or an adverb of your own. Write the new sentence.

impressively	cautiously	always
really	outside	suddenly

1. Jonah practices Korean martial arts in the mornings.

_____

_____

2. He likes *tae kwon do.*

_____

3. Jonah kicks his legs.

_____

4. Jonah and the other class members jump.

_____

5. The teacher uses his feet.

_____

6. In warm weather, students practice in the courtyard.

_____

_____

Directions Write two sentences about actions you do in a sport or activity. Use at least two adverbs. Underline the adverbs.

_____

_____

Home Activity Your child learned how to use adverbs in writing. Have your child write a postcard to a friend or family member and include an adverb in the message.

Grammar and Writing Practice Book

Adverbs

Directions Mark the letter of the word that is an adverb.

1. It rains heavily in Korea in winter.
   A rains
   B heavily
   C in
   D winter

2. The monsoon wind blows powerfully.
   A monsoon
   B wind
   C blows
   D powerfully

3. The rice grows quickly in the wet fields.
   A grows
   B rice
   C quickly
   D wet

4. Farmers soon plant some vegetables.
   A soon
   B plant
   C vegetables
   D some

5. Fishermen work there on the coasts.
   A work
   B there
   C on
   D coasts

6. They catch many kinds of fish easily.
   A catch
   B fish
   C many
   D easily

7. Some farmers grow oranges yearly.
   A grow
   B some
   C yearly
   D oranges

8. They patiently raise chickens and pigs.
   A patiently
   B raise
   C chickens
   D pigs

9. Today Korea produces much food.
   A Today
   B produces
   C much
   D food

10. Korea surely has many resources.
    A Korea
    B many
    C surely
    D has

Home Activity Your child prepared for taking tests on adverbs. While reading a book with your child, have him or her describe the actions in a picture using two adverbs in the description.

Adverbs

Directions Underline the adverb in each sentence.

1. Often, moving to a new country is difficult.

2. You must leave your friends behind.

3. The houses are built differently.

4. The people dress strangely.

5. Soon you like your new home.

Directions Choose the correct word in ( ) to complete each sentence. Write the new sentence.

6. Kim's grandpa lived (peacefully, peaceful) with Kim's family in Korea.

_____

_____

7. Kim's grandpa moved (cheerful, cheerfully) to America with the family.

_____

_____

8. He (kindly, kind) tells Kim a story each night.

_____

9. He (usually, usual) tells stories about life in Korea.

_____

10. Kim looks forward (excited, excitedly) to her grandpa's stories.

_____

 Home Activity Your child reviewed adverbs. While playing actively, have your child demonstrate the following movements: running slowly, crawling quietly, and walking carefully.

Grammar and Writing Practice Book

Adverbs That Compare

> You can use **adverbs** to compare actions. The *-er* form of an adverb compares two actions. The *-est* form of an adverb compares three or more actions.
>
>   Jeremy works <u>hard</u>.
>   Jeremy works <u>harder</u> than Tom does.
>   Jeremy works <u>hardest</u> of all the students.
>
> Most adverbs that end in *-ly* use *more* and *most* to make comparisons.
>   The truck moved <u>slowly</u>.
>   The truck moved <u>more slowly</u> than the car.
>   The truck moved <u>most slowly</u> of all.

Directions Underline the adverb that compares in each sentence.

1. Mrs. Alvarez sings the loudest of all the employees at the bakery.

2. She bakes faster than Mr. Lane does.

3. The bread dough rises most quickly of all.

4. You must knead bread dough more carefully than other kinds of dough.

5. Mrs. Alvarez has been baking longer than you have.

Directions Circle the correct word in ( ) to complete each sentence.

6. The muffins bake (slower, slowest) than the cinnamon rolls.

7. Mr. Costa works the (faster, fastest) of all the bakers.

8. Of all the workers, Tony sings (more cheerfully, most cheerfully).

9. Mr. Costa mixes sweet roll dough (most rapidly, more rapidly) than Tony.

10. The sweet rolls are done (sooner, soonest) of all.

© Pearson Education, Inc. 3

Home Activity Your child learned about adverbs that compare. Ask your child to compare how he or she rides a bicycle to the way a friend rides, using an adverb that compares.

Name _____

Adverbs That Compare

Directions Answer each question. Use a comparative or superlative form of an adverb in the box or an adverb of your own in each answer.

> quickly   soon   hard   long   slowly

1. How hard did Carlos and Tara work in cooking class compared to all the other students?

   _____

   _____

2. How long did Carlos stay in the kitchen compared to Tara?

   _____

3. How quickly did Tara mix her cake batter compared to all the other students?

   _____

   _____

4. How soon was Tara's cake done compared to Carlos's cake?

   _____

5. How slowly did Tara's cake rise compared to all the other students' cakes?

   _____

Directions Write two sentences about experiences you have had helping in the kitchen. Use two adverbs that compare. You may use adverbs from the box above or think of your own. Underline the adverbs.

_____

_____

_____

Home Activity Your child learned how to use adverbs that compare in writing. Have your child write two sentences giving advice about cooking or another activity to someone younger. Have your child use at least one adverb that compares in the sentences.

Grammar and Writing Practice Book

Name _____

Adverbs That Compare

Directions Mark the letter of the word that correctly completes each sentence.

1. Polly's alarm rings _____ than mine does.
   A loudest
   B loudly
   C loud
   D louder

2. She is getting up _____ today than yesterday.
   A more cheerfully
   B cheerful
   C most cheerful
   D more cheerfuller

3. She will get to the food fair the _____ of anyone.
   A soon
   B more soon
   C sooner
   D soonest

4. The fair will last _____ this year than last year.
   A longly
   B longer
   C long
   D longest

5. Polly will work the _____ of anyone at the fair.
   A hardest
   B hard
   C harder
   D most hard

6. Of all the workers, she will work _____.
   A more quickly
   B quicker
   C most quickly
   D quick

7. She will try new foods _____ than Tim will.
   A eagerly
   B most eagerly
   C more eagerer
   D more eagerly

8. She will eat good foods _____ than her friend.
   A fast
   B more fast
   C fastest
   D faster

© Pearson Education, Inc. 3

Home Activity Your child prepared for taking tests on adverbs that compare. While working in the kitchen with your child, ask him or her to make up a sentence about cooking that includes an adverb that compares.

Grammar and Writing Practice Book

Adverbs That Compare

Directions Underline the adverb that compares in each sentence.

1. Thomas makes pizza dough faster than Kenneth.

2. Kenneth makes sandwiches more quickly than Thomas.

3. Michael prepares salads the earliest of all the chefs.

4. The sandwich is done sooner than the pizza.

5. Which of the three boys worked the longest at Mr. King's restaurant?

6. Of the three boys, Michael works most carefully.

Directions Circle the correct word in ( ) to complete each sentence.

7. Of all the students, George worked on his speech the (harder, hardest).

8. Jay speaks (loudest, louder) than Katie.

9. Katie speaks (more quietly, most quietly) than the teacher.

10. George talked (more excitedly, most excitedly) of all the speakers.

11. Jay talked (longer, longest) than Katie did.

12. Katie spoke the (slower, slowest) of all the students.

© Pearson Education, Inc. 3

Home Activity Your child reviewed adverbs that compare. While driving in the car, have your child compare the actions of some other cars by using the verb *move* and the following words: *faster, fastest, slower, slowest.*

Name _____

Conjunctions

A **conjunction** is a word that connects words or groups of words.

- To add information, use the conjunction *and*. To show a choice, use the conjunction *or*. To show a difference, use the conjunction *but*.

  James went to the park <u>and</u> a ball game.
  James had never been to New York City, <u>but</u> he liked it.
  James could stay in the city <u>or</u> go back home.

- You can use a conjunction to combine two sentences into a compound sentence. Add a comma before the conjunction in a compound sentence.

  James went to a ball game. Then he went home.
  James went to a ball game, and then he went home.

Directions Write the conjunction in each sentence.

1. Railroads were built in the 1800s, and Americans soon depended on them. _____

2. Americans could travel by stagecoach, but trains were much faster. _____

3. People could go 20 miles or all the way across country. _____

4. Today Americans travel by airplanes, cars, and trains. _____

5. You can take a train within a city or between cities. _____

Directions Circle the conjunction in ( ) that best completes each sentence.

6. Daniel saw the Statue of Liberty (but, and) the Empire State Building.

7. Was the Statue of Liberty dedicated in 1884 (or, but) 1886?

8. It was sent to the United States in 1884, (or, but) it was dedicated in 1886.

9. Is the statue made of copper (but, or) marble?

10. The statue was cleaned (but, and) restored in the 1980s.

School-Home CONNECTION

Home Activity Your child learned about conjunctions. Ask your child to name his or her favorite things to do after school, using one or more conjunctions.

© Pearson Education, Inc.3

Name _____

Conjunctions

Directions Combine each pair of sentences using the conjunction shown. In combining the pairs, use the underlined repeated words and phrases only once. Make any necessary changes in words. Add a comma in compound sentences.

Example You can see art in a museum. You can see art in a gallery. (or)

You can see art in a museum or gallery.

1. The Empire State Building is a famous skyscraper. The Chrysler Building is a famous skyscraper. (and)

_____

_____

2. New York City has many parks. James likes Central Park best. (but)

_____

_____

3. Visitors can go to a baseball game. Visitors can go to a basketball game. (or)

_____

_____

Directions Write two short, related sentences about a city you have visited. Then combine the sentences using a conjunction. Remember to add a comma.

_____

_____

_____

_____

Home Activity Your child learned how to use conjunctions in writing. Have your child write two short, related sentences about a recent special occasion in your family. Have your child combine the sentences using a conjunction.

© Pearson Education, Inc. 3

Capital Letters

Use **capital letters** for proper nouns. Proper nouns include days of the week, months of the year, and holidays. Titles for people should be capitalized when they are used with a person's name. Do not capitalize titles when they are used by themselves.

Incorrect	Last october aunt Rosie and my Uncle gave a party for halloween.
Correct	Last October Aunt Rosie and my uncle gave a party for Halloween.
Incorrect	Does mother's day come earlier than memorial day?
Correct	Does Mother's Day come earlier than Memorial Day?

Directions Write correctly the words that should have capital letters.

1. Last may Mara saw some wonderful sights.

_____

2. Mara's mom and aunt lucy took her to the Statue of Liberty.

_____

3. They saw the Liberty Bell in philadelphia on memorial day.

_____

Directions Write the sentences. Use capital letters correctly.

4. Bartholdi hoped the statue would be finished by july 4, 1876.

_____

_____

5. Only the statue's arm and torch were ready by the fourth of july.

_____

_____

Home Activity Your child learned about capital letters. While looking at a magazine, ask your child to point out three capital letters used for days of the week, months of the year, or holidays.

Capital Letters

Directions Complete each sentence with a proper noun for the word in ( ). Use capital letters correctly.

1. One of my favorite holidays is _____. (holiday)

2. We celebrate this holiday in _____. (month)

3. This year my birthday is on _____. (day of the week)

4. The day of the week that I like best is _____. (day of the week)

5. I like the weather in the month of _____. (month)

6. I do not like the weather in the month of _____. (month)

Directions Write two sentences about something you do with family members on a particular holiday. Use capital letters correctly.

_____

_____

_____

_____

_____

_____

_____

_____

© Pearson Education, Inc.3

Home Activity Your child learned how to use capital letters in writing. With your child, recall an event that included many family members. Have your child write a list of the people, using capital letters correctly.

Name _____

Capital Letters

Directions Mark the letter of the word or words that should be capitalized.

1. The family sailed across the ocean in february.
   A family
   B across
   C ocean
   D february

2. On monday the children said good-bye to their grandparents.
   A monday
   B good-bye
   C children
   D grandparents

3. On friday the ship arrived in a new country.
   A ship
   B friday
   C country
   D new

4. The next day aunt sue took her guests to the city.
   A next day
   B aunt sue
   C guests
   D city

5. Their aunt told the family about holidays in america.
   A aunt
   B holidays
   C family
   D america

6. She said people enjoy fireworks on independence day.
   A people
   B independence
   C independence day
   D fireworks

7. Americans remember explorers on columbus day.
   A explorers
   B voyages
   C remember
   D columbus day

8. I hope Grandpa visits us at hanukkah.
   A hope
   B visits
   C us
   D hanukkah

© Pearson Education, Inc.3

Home Activity Your child prepared for taking tests on capital letters. Look at a calendar with your child and have him or her point out capital letters and explain the reasons for their use.

Grammar and Writing Practice Book

Unit 6 Week 1 **103**

Capital Letters

Directions If a sentence has capitalization mistakes, write correctly the words that should have capital letters. If a sentence has no capitalization mistakes, write *C*.

1. The Statue of Liberty was repaired in the 1980s. _____

2. In our town, mr. barnes raised money for the repairs. _____

3. Many Americans helped keep the statue on Liberty Island beautiful.

    _____

4. People celebrated the restored statue on the fourth of july in 1986.

    _____

5. They also celebrated in october, 100 years after the original dedication.

    _____

Directions Write the sentences. Use capital letters correctly.

6. On monday, the class read poems about freedom.

    _____

    _____

7. A poem by emma lazarus appears on the statue of liberty.

    _____

    _____

8. Our teacher, ms. adams, says it inspires people from around the world.

    _____

    _____

Home Activity Your child reviewed capital letters. While outdoors, have your child write the name of a day of the week with correct capitalization using natural objects, such as sand, twigs, or pebbles.

© Pearson Education, Inc. 3

Abbreviations

An **abbreviation** is a shortened form of a word. Many abbreviations begin with a capital letter and end with a period.

- Some titles used for names of people are abbreviations. For example, *Dr.* is the abbreviation for *Doctor*. The title *Miss* is not abbreviated.

  Mr. Don Lee Chang   Ms. Lucy Ruiz   Mrs. Maya Levin

- An **initial** is the first letter of a name. It is written with a capital letter and is followed by a period.

  Mr. Don L. Chang   L. T. Ruiz   M. E. Levin

- The names of days and months can be abbreviated. *May, June,* and *July* are not abbreviated.

  Days of the Week
  Sun.   Mon.   Tues.   Wed.   Thurs.   Fri.   Sat.
  Months of the Year
  Jan.   Feb.   Mar.   Apr.   Aug.   Sept.   Oct.   Nov.   Dec.

Directions Write each abbreviation. Be sure to capitalize letters and use periods correctly.

1. Mrs W. Wenders   _____

2. j r Burton   _____

3. sat, aug 4   _____

4. ms T j. Matthews   _____

Directions Some abbreviations can be used in sentences. Find the word that can be abbreviated in the sentence below. Write the sentence with the abbreviation.

5. Mister Alexis got a pet bird when he moved to this country.

_____

_____

Home Activity Your child learned about abbreviations. Look through the mail with your child. Have him or her identify abbreviations used for people's names and titles.

© Pearson Education, Inc. 3

Abbreviations

Directions Write the answer to each question. Use abbreviations correctly.

1. What are your initials?

_____

2. What is the abbreviation for the month in which you were born?

_____

3. What are the titles and last names of the adults in your family?

_____

4. What is the abbreviation for your busiest day of the week?

_____

5. What is the abbreviation for the month in which your favorite holiday takes place?

_____

6. What is the abbreviation for today's day of the week?

_____

Directions Write two sentences about two adults besides your parents who have taught you important skills or lessons. Use at least two abbreviations.

_____

_____

_____

_____

_____

Home Activity Your child learned how to use abbreviations in writing. With your child, list some adults who live in your neighborhood. Have your child write their names, using the correct abbreviations for their titles.

Abbreviations

Directions Mark the letter of the correct abbreviation for each word.

1. Monday
  A mon
  B Mon
  C mon.
  D Mon.

2. Mister
  A mr.
  B Mr.
  C Mr
  D mr

3. April
  A Apr.
  B apr
  C apr.
  D Apr

4. Wednesday
  A wed.
  B wed
  C Wed
  D Wed.

5. February
  A feb
  B Feb
  C Feb.
  D feb.

6. Doctor
  A dr
  B Dr
  C dr.
  D Dr.

7. Richard James
  A RJ.
  B rj.
  C R. J.
  D r. j.

8. August
  A aug
  B Aug.
  C Aug
  D aug.

9. Saturday
  A sat.
  B sat
  C Sat.
  D Sat

10. October
  A oct
  B Oct.
  C Oct
  D oct.

© Pearson Education, Inc. 3

Home Activity Your child prepared for taking tests on abbreviations. Have your child write the days of the week, using abbreviations correctly.

Abbreviations

Directions Write each sentence correctly. Use correct capitalization and periods for abbreviations.

1. Dr and mrs Hartz have many beautiful pet birds.

_____

2. They will display the birds at the home of mr and Ms Santos.

_____

_____

3. I am going to see the birds with my friend c. j. Fox.

_____

4. You can buy tickets at G B Watkins Department Store.

_____

_____

Directions The following research notes have initials and abbreviations written incorrectly. Write each note. Correct mistakes in initials and abbreviations.

5. John j Audubon—bird painter

_____

6. Born apr 1785

_____

7. Wrote book about animals with J Bachman

_____

8. Died jan 1851

_____

Home Activity Your child reviewed abbreviations. Scan a newspaper with your child and have your child identify abbreviations.

Combining Sentences

When you **combine sentences,** you join two sentences that are about the same topic. You make them into one sentence.

- You can join two simple sentences and make a compound sentence. Add a comma and a conjunction such as *and, but,* or *or.*

  Jen drew a tree. I drew a bird. Jen drew a tree, and I drew a bird.

- You can combine two sentences that have the same subject.

  Jen got blue paint. Jen painted the sky. Jen got blue paint and painted the sky.

- You can combine two sentences that have the same predicate.

  Jen painted. I painted. Jen and I painted.

- You can combine two sentences by using an appositive.

  We made a mural. A mural is a wall painting. We made a mural, a wall painting.

- You can combine two sentences by using adjectives or adverbs.

  That mural is big. Our mural is bigger. Our mural is bigger than that mural.
  We painted the mural. We painted it quickly. We painted the mural quickly.

- You can combine two sentences by using prepositional phrases.

  They saw the mural. It was on Main Street. They saw the mural on Main Street.

Directions Combine each pair of sentences into a compound sentence. Use a comma and the conjunction in ( ).

1. Some murals show famous people. Our mural shows ordinary people. (but)

  _____

  _____

2. I will show you the mural. You can find it yourself. (or)

  _____

  _____

Directions Combine the sentences. Use the underlined words only once in the new sentence.

3. Diego Rivera came from Mexico. Diego Rivera painted murals in America.

  _____

  _____

Home Activity Your child learned about combining sentences. Point out two short related sentences in a book you are reading with your child. Have your child combine the sentences.

Combining Sentences

Directions Combine each pair of simple sentences into a compound sentence. Add a comma and the conjunction *and, but,* or *or.*

1. People painted murals long ago. They still paint murals today.

_____

_____

2. Some murals are painted outside. Most murals are painted inside.

_____

_____

3. You can make a mural with paint. You can use bits of glass.

_____

_____

4. One artist can make a mural. Many artists can work together.

_____

_____

Directions Write two simple related sentences about murals. Then combine the sentences to make one compound sentence.

_____

_____

_____

_____

Home Activity Your child learned how to combine sentences in writing. Have your child write two short sentences on the same topic on construction paper, cut them out, and combine them on another sheet of paper, adding a comma and a conjunction such as *and.*

Combining Sentences

Directions Mark the letter of the words that complete each sentence correctly.

1. Julia planned a _____ painted it.
   A mural, And the class
   B mural, or the class
   C mural, and the class
   D mural and the class

2. The mural is about our _____ is so interesting.
   A town, And it
   B town, and it
   C town, or it
   D town and it

3. The mural is not _____ has many scenes.
   A huge, but it
   B huge, But it
   C huge but it
   D huge, or it

4. Tim _____ painted the park.
   A and Lee
   B , and Lee
   C and, Lee
   D and Lee,

5. You can use yellow _____ can use red.
   A paint, Or you
   B paint or you
   C paint, or you
   D paint but you

6. The pictures are _____ bright.
   A big, and
   B big, and
   C , big and
   D big and

7. You can paint a _____ can paint a house.
   A tree but you
   B tree or you
   C tree, Or you
   D tree, or you

8. People look at the _____ love it.
   A mural, or they
   B mural, and they
   C mural, And they
   D mural and they

9. The mural was hard _____ was worth it.
   A work, but it
   B work but it
   C work, But it
   D work or it

10. We will paint a mural next _____ will be even better.
    A year but it
    B year, And it
    C year, and it
    D year and it

Home Activity Your child prepared for taking tests on combining sentences. Have your child show you pairs of short related sentences from a school paper and explain how to combine them.

Combining Sentences

Directions Combine each pair of sentences. Use the way shown in ( ).

1. Many painters create murals. Murals are a popular art form. (appositive)

_____

_____

2. You can paint a mural on canvas. You can use oil paints. (prepositional phrase)

_____

_____

3. The people gazed at the mural. They were excited. (adverb)

_____

_____

Directions Combine each pair of sentences. Use the underlined words only once in your new sentence.

4. That mural shows many different people. That mural pictures several events.

_____

_____

5. A mural can entertain people. A mural can teach people.

_____

_____

6. Public buildings are good places for murals. Parks are good places for murals.

_____

_____

Home Activity Your child reviewed combining sentences. While looking at a magazine or newspaper, ask your child to combine pairs of related sentences in two different ways.

© Pearson Education, Inc. 3

Grammar and Writing Practice Book

Commas

Use a **comma** and a conjunction to join two sentences.

There was a crumb on the table, and the ant crawled toward it.

Use **commas** to separate words in a series.

We had sandwiches, cookies, and fruit at the picnic.

Use a **comma** after the greeting and the closing of a friendly letter.

Dear Jake,

Your friend,

Use a **comma** between the name of a city and a state in an address.

Chico, CA 95926   Berea, Kentucky

Use a **comma** to separate the month and day from the year.

July 21, 2006

Directions Write *C* if commas are used correctly in the sentence. Write *NC* if commas are not used correctly.

1. Some kinds of ants are army ants, honey ants, and dairying ants. _____

2. Army ants travel in lines and they hunt other insects. _____

3. Dear Amy _____

Directions Write each sentence. Add commas where they are needed.

4. Some ants eat other insects but many do not.

_____

_____

5. The newspaper had an article about ants on November 14 2005.

_____

_____

Home Activity Your child learned about commas. Have your child point out five commas in a book that you are reading together.

Commas

Directions Answer each question with a complete sentence. Make your writing clear by using commas correctly.

1. In what city and state do you live?

_____

_____

2. What month, day, and year were you born?

_____

_____

3. What are three of your favorite colors?

_____

_____

4. What are three of your favorite foods?

_____

_____

5. What are two activities you do in your free time? Answer with a compound sentence.

_____

_____

Directions Write a sentence listing three traits of ants. Use commas correctly.

_____

_____

Home Activity Your child learned how to use commas in writing. Have your child write a sentence naming three animals that he or she likes, using commas correctly.

Grammar and Writing Practice Book

Commas

Directions Mark the letter of the words that complete the sentence correctly.

1. The ants march along _____.
   A grass, bushes, and trees
   B grass bushes and trees
   C grass, bushes and trees
   D grass bushes, and trees

2. The ants carry _____.
   A crumbs, salt and sugar
   B crumbs salt and sugar
   C crumbs, salt, and sugar
   D crumbs salt, and sugar

3. Some ants _____ lay eggs.
   A work and others
   B work, and others
   C work, And others
   D work And others

4. The ants are _____.
   A red black and brown
   B red, black and brown
   C red black, and brown
   D red, black, and brown

5. I drew these ants on _____.
   A March 8 2005
   B March, 8, 2005
   C March 8, 2005
   D March 8 2005,

6. I saw many ants in _____.
   A Atlanta Georgia
   B Atlanta, Georgia
   C Atlanta, Georgia,
   D Atlanta Georgia,

7. We had a picnic with _____.
   A salad, fruit, and juice
   B salad fruit and juice
   C salad, fruit and juice
   D salad fruit, and juice

8. Some _____ came to the picnic too.
   A ants bees and flies
   B ants bees, and flies
   C ants, bees and flies
   D ants, bees, and flies

9. Bees _____ crawled.
   A flew and ants
   B flew, and ants
   C flew, And ants
   D flew And ants

10. I like _____ doesn't.
    A insects but Rob
    B insects, But Rob
    C insects But Rob
    D insects, but Rob

Home Activity Your child prepared for taking tests on commas. Have your child show you some sentences from a school paper or ad and explain why they need commas or not.

Grammar and Writing Practice Book

Commas

Directions Fix the comma errors in the sentences in the letter. If a phrase or sentence does not have a comma error, write *C*.

1. Dear Lisa

_____

2. We looked at ants bees and butterflies in science class.

_____

3. I love butterflies but I am not crazy about ants.

_____

4. Tomorrow we will study frogs lizards and snakes.

_____

Directions Write each sentence. Add commas where they are needed.

5. My brother went to camp on July 10 2005.

_____

_____

6. He loves insects and he was happy to live in a tent.

_____

_____

7. In his tent he saw spiders ants and flies.

_____

_____

Home Activity Your child reviewed commas. Have your child look at letters and envelopes in the mail and point out commas used in dates and addresses.

Grammar and Writing Practice Book

Quotations and Parentheses

Quotation marks (" ") show the exact words of a speaker in a conversation.

- Use a comma to separate the speaker's exact words from the rest of the sentence.
- Use a capital letter to begin the first words inside the quotation marks.
- Put the punctuation mark that ends the quotation inside the quotation marks.

  "I can play music on my pipe," said Elena.

  She asked, "Shall I play for you?"

Quotation marks also indicate many kinds of titles, such as song, poem, story, and document titles.

  We read "Elena's Serenade."

Parentheses show explanations or examples that are extra information.

  That song (written in 1996) is my favorite.

  Some singers (for example, Elton John) play the piano too.

Directions Underline the part of each sentence that is a quotation.

 1. "I want to play the flute," said Jeremy.

 2. "I will teach you," replied Ms. Foster.

 3. Ms. Foster said, "Everyone will enjoy your songs."

Directions Write the sentences. Add quotation marks and commas where they are needed.

 4. Some of my songs are happy said Jeremy.

 _____

 5. Ms. Foster exclaimed You play beautifully!

 _____

 6. Jeremy can play a song named Paco's Dog.

 _____

Home Activity Your child learned about quotations. Have your child read aloud a quotation in a book you are reading together and then point out each punctuation mark and explain the reason for it.

Quotations and Parentheses

Directions Write a quotation in a sentence to answer each question. Use *I replied, I answered, I said,* and *I exclaimed*.

1. "What is your favorite kind of music?" Jeremy asked.

_____

2. "What musical instrument would you like to play?" Nicole asked.

_____

Directions Add an explanation or example in parentheses to each sentence. Write the new sentence.

3. Some songs are fun to sing along with others.

_____

_____

4. Some instruments are very hard to learn.

_____

_____

Directions Imagine a conversation you might have with a friend about learning to play a musical instrument. Write three sentences of the conversation. Use quotation marks and other punctuation correctly. Use at least one sentence that gives extra information in parentheses.

_____

_____

_____

_____

Home Activity Your child learned how to use quotations and parentheses in writing. Have your child write a quotation from a conversation you had during the day. Make sure your child uses correct punctuation marks.

Grammar and Writing Practice Book

Quotations and Parentheses

Directions Mark the letter of the words that should go inside quotation marks.

1. The desert is great, Tim said.

 A Tim said

 B The desert

 C The desert is great,

 D The desert is great, Tim

2. Look at the cactus, I responded.

 A Look

 B Look at the cactus,

 C I

 D I said

3. Tim said, There are bushes too.

 A Tim said,

 B Tim said, There

 C There are

 D There are bushes too.

4. I said, There is not much water.

 A There is not much water.

 B I said, There

 C There is not

 D not much water.

5. It is hot and dry, Tim exclaimed.

 A Tim said.

 B It is hot and dry,

 C It is hot

 D hot and dry, Tim

6. Do animals live here? I asked.

 A Do animals live here?

 B Do animals?

 C live here? I asked

 D I asked.

7. Some like hot weather, Tim said.

 A hot weather, Tim said.

 B Some like

 C Some like hot weather,

 D Tim said.

8. I said, I like it too.

 A I said,

 B I like

 C I said, I like

 D I like it too.

Home Activity Your child prepared for taking tests on quotations. Have your child identify words in quotation marks in a newspaper article and explain why they are punctuated in that way.

Quotations and Parentheses

Directions Write *C* if a sentence is correct. If it is not correct, make the corrections that are needed.

1. Mr. Sanchez said, "You can make beautiful glass by blowing. _____

2. "It is an interesting art," said Julio. _____

3. You use a blowpipe to make a glass ball," Mr. Sanchez added. _____

4. It looks really hard! Carla exclaimed. _____

5. Glassblowing takes a lot of practice," Mr. Sanchez said. _____

Directions Write each sentence. Add a comma and quotation marks where they are needed.

6. People have been blowing glass for thousands of years Ms. Rice said.

_____

_____

7. Glassmakers used big furnaces in the 1700s added Ms. Rice.

_____

_____

Directions Write each sentence. Draw a line under the word or words that are explained by the phrases in parentheses.

8. The blowpipe was invented long ago (in 30 B.C.).

_____

9. Colonists built a glass factory in Jamestown (America's first permanent English colony) in 1608.

_____

_____

Home Activity Your child reviewed quotations. With your child, read aloud a conversation between two or more characters in a favorite storybook and point out and explain the punctuation marks in the dialogue.

Grammar and Writing Practice Book

Grammar
Cumulative Review

Sentences

Directions Read the groups of words. Write the group of words that is a sentence.

1. We play many computer games.
   Other kinds of games too.

   _____

2. High winds and heavy rain.
   A big storm blows power lines down.

   _____

3. We don't need power for board games.
   Played checkers all day.

   _____

4. Some kids got bored.
   No power to play video games.

   _____

5. Finished an art project.
   My friends painted a mural.

   _____

Directions Decide whether each group of words is a sentence or a fragment.
If it is a sentence, write the sentence with correct capitalization and punctuation.
If it is a fragment, write *F*.

6. we can play tag and soccer outdoors

   _____

7. people on the baseball field

   _____

8. looked everywhere for a battery

   _____

9. they discovered new games during the storm

   _____

Subjects and Predicates

Directions Underline the complete subject of each sentence.

1. Mom needs help around the house.

2. My little brother needs attention.

3. Everyone in the family needs something.

4. Each person helps the others.

5. All of us think of the needs of others.

Directions Write the complete predicate of each sentence.

6. Julie cooks soup for dinner.

   _____

7. I wash the car with Dad.

   _____

8. My brother picks up his toys.

   _____

9. Each family member has a special job.

   _____

10. Life at my house goes more smoothly this way.

   _____

Statements and Questions

Directions Write *statement* if the sentence is a statement. Write *question* if the sentence is a question.

1. Fish is a tasty, healthful food. _____

2. What is your favorite kind of fish? _____

3. Fish tastes good with all kinds of spices. _____

4. How shall we cook this big trout? _____

5. We can make tacos or soup with it. _____

Directions Write the sentences. Add the correct end punctuation. Write *S* if the sentence is a statement and *Q* if the sentence is a question.

6. Can we fish in this pond

_____

7. Has anyone caught anything

_____

8. The fish leap out of the water

_____

9. There are big fish and little fish

_____

10. Did you see that colorful fish

_____

11. It is tugging on my line

_____

12. How much does it weigh

_____

Commands and Exclamations

Directions Write *command* if the sentence is a command, or imperative sentence.
Write *exclamation* if the sentence is an exclamation, or an exclamatory sentence.

1. Please buy some fruit. _____

2. What big strawberries those are! _____

3. Try some grapefruit. _____

4. The peaches are delicious! _____

Directions Write the sentences. Add the correct end punctuation. Write *C* if the
sentence is a command and *E* if the sentence is an exclamation.

5. Go to the supermarket

_____

6. Get food for lunch

_____

7. What a big choice there is

_____

8. Don't forget the lettuce

_____

9. This turkey tastes too spicy

_____

10. Find some American cheese

_____

11. I love sandwiches

_____

12. My lunch will be great

_____

© Pearson Education, Inc. 3

Compound Sentences

Directions Write *S* if the sentence is a simple sentence. Write *C* if the sentence is a compound sentence.

1. Many people use bicycles for their jobs.   _____

2. Some people deliver messages on their bikes.   _____

3. James carries flowers on his bike, and Dave carries groceries. _____

4. Dave prefers heavy loads, but it is hard work.   _____

5. Bicycles are fun, and they are also useful.   _____

Directions Use the word *and, but,* or *or* to combine each pair of sentences. Write the compound sentence.

6. Kevin worked hard. He saved money for a skateboard.

_____

_____

7. The store had many skateboards. Kevin wanted a special one.

_____

_____

8. You buy a skateboard from the store. You order one from a catalog.

_____

_____

9. Kevin found the perfect skateboard in a catalog. He ordered it right away.

_____

_____

10. Kevin waited a long time for his skateboard. It was worth the wait.

_____

_____

Name _____

Common and Proper Nouns

Directions Write *C* if the underlined noun is a common noun. Write *P* if the underlined noun is a proper noun.

1. Antarctica is an unusual <u>continent</u>.   _____

2. The <u>South Pole</u> is found there.   _____

3. The <u>weather</u> is harsh.   _____

4. It is one of the coldest places in the <u>world</u>.   _____

5. Yet some animals build <u>nests</u> on the land.   _____

6. The islands of <u>Antarctica</u> are home to many birds.   _____

7. Some <u>birds</u> live on the ocean.   _____

8. They find <u>fish</u> for food.   _____

9. Interesting birds live along the seashore of <u>America</u>. _____

10. Gulls and terns nest on the <u>coast</u> and fish at sea.   _____

Directions Underline the common nouns and circle the proper nouns in the sentences.

11. Ducks and geese make nests near the North Pole.

12. The animals come to the shores of North America in winter.

13. Many gulls live near the ocean in Canada.

14. They follow ships and eat trash that people throw out.

15. These birds also live on the Great Lakes.

Singular and Plural Nouns

Direction Write *S* if the underlined noun is singular. Write *P* if the underlined noun is plural.

1. It is a hot day in the <u>field</u>. _____

2. The <u>workers</u> must stop for a break. _____

3. They have picked many <u>grapes</u>. _____

4. They put the <u>boxes</u> on the truck. _____

5. We will buy the fruit at the <u>store</u>. _____

Directions Write the plural nouns in each sentence.

6. The farmers planted pumpkins in their fields.

_____

7. The plants grew in long rows.

_____

8. In September the corn stalks were huge.

_____

9. Workers picked the ripe vegetables.

_____

10. Students took trips on buses.

_____

11. Boys and girls picked apples.

_____

12. Farms are busy places in the fall.

_____

Grammar and Writing Practice Book

Irregular Plural Nouns

Directions Write *S* if the underlined noun is singular. Write *P* if the underlined noun is plural.

1. The <u>women</u> next door had a problem in their barn. _____

2. Some <u>mice</u> had made homes there. _____

3. The little animals bothered the big <u>oxen</u> in the barn. _____

4. A noisy <u>goose</u> went into the barn. _____

5. Soon there were no mice under the people's <u>feet</u>. _____

Directions Write the plural nouns in each sentence.

6. The children had problems.

   _____

7. They had loose teeth.

   _____

8. They could not eat apples or carrots.

   _____

9. Soon their teeth fell out, and their mouths felt better.

   _____

10. They could eat snacks again.

    _____

Singular Possessive Nouns

Directions Write the singular possessive noun in each sentence.

1. The little hen used the farmer's wheat for bread.

_____

2. The hen asked for each animal's help.

_____

3. Each friend's answer was no.

_____

4. The animals wanted the hen's good bread.

_____

5. The hen enjoyed the bread's taste alone.

_____

Directions Write the possessive form of the underlined singular noun in each sentence.

6. What is that <u>story</u> lesson?

_____

7. Good bread comes from the <u>baker</u> hard work.

_____

8. Everyone wants the <u>worker</u> food.

_____

9. No one helps in the <u>cook</u> kitchen.

_____

10. Each <u>person</u> help is needed.

_____

Grammar and Writing Practice Book

Plural Possessive Nouns

Directions Write the plural possessive noun in each sentence.

1. The chicks' fur is so soft.

   _____

2. Hummingbirds' bills are long and thin.

   _____

3. Weaver birds' nests are cleverly built.

   _____

4. The robins' eggs lie safely in nests.

   _____

5. Building nests is the females' job.

   _____

Directions Write the possessive form of the underlined plural noun in each sentence.

6. The students saw <u>eagles</u> nests in the treetops.

   _____

7. They found <u>woodpeckers</u> eggs in tree trunks.

   _____

8. Take pictures of some <u>sparrows</u> nests.

   _____

9. Look carefully at the <u>nests</u> materials.

   _____

10. Some <u>animals</u> homes are lined with feathers.

    _____

11. The <u>feathers</u> colors are black and brown.

    _____

12. The <u>students</u> day was full of interesting sights.

    _____

Name _____

Action and Linking Verbs

Directions Write the verb in each sentence.

1. Grandma plants bulbs every fall. _____

2. The plants grow in spring. _____

3. That plant is a lily. _____

4. These lilies are white. _____

5. This bulb is a tulip. _____

6. Everyone loves Grandma's flowers. _____

Directions Write the verb in each sentence. Write *A* after an action verb. Write *L* after a linking verb.

7. Peter waters the garden each day. _____

8. The flowers need special care. _____

9. Jamal pulls weeds each week. _____

10. The flowers are prettier than ever this year. _____

11. The summer rain is important for the flowers. _____

12. Jessica picks flowers for a special occasion. _____

13. She arranges roses in a vase. _____

14. The vase is on the table. _____

15. Mom enjoys the flowers. _____

16. She thanks Jessica for the gift. _____

17. Roses are her favorite flowers. _____

18. Dad takes a picture. _____

Grammar and Writing Practice Book

Main Verbs and Helping Verbs

Directions Write the main verb and the helping verb in each sentence.

1. The men are hunting for deer in the forest.

   Main verb: _____

   Helping verb: _____

2. The women have planted corn in the field.

   Main verb: _____

   Helping verb: _____

3. The boys were fishing in the clear lake.

   Main verb: _____

   Helping verb: _____

4. The girl has sewn a pretty dress.

   Main verb: _____

   Helping verb: _____

5. I am learning about Native American life.

   Main verb: _____

   Helping verb: _____

Directions Look at the underlined verb in each sentence. Write *M* if it is a main verb. Write *H* if it is a helping verb.

6. A woman was <u>weaving</u> a basket. _____

7. She <u>will</u> make a necklace with beads. _____

8. The girls had <u>cut</u> the deerskin in pieces. _____

9. They are <u>making</u> shoes for everyone. _____

10. The boy <u>is</u> gathering pretty feathers. _____

© Pearson Education, Inc.3

Subject-Verb Agreement

Direction Choose the verb in ( ) that agrees with the subject. Write the verb.

1. The city lights (hide, hides) the stars. _____

2. Stars (gleam, gleams) brightly in the country. _____

3. They (seem, seems) close enough to touch. _____

4. The Big Dipper (look, looks) huge. _____

5. Our galaxy (is, are) amazing. _____

Directions Choose the verb in ( ) that agrees with the subject. Write the sentence.

6. This telescope (work, works) well.

_____

_____

7. We (see, sees) millions of stars.

_____

_____

8. Rigel (is, are) one of the brightest stars.

_____

_____

9. Hot gases (make, makes) it sparkle.

_____

_____

10. Astronomers often (find, finds) new stars.

_____

_____

Grammar and Writing Practice Book

Present, Past, and Future Tenses

Directions Tell the tense of the underlined verb in each sentence. Write *present*, *past*, or *future*.

1. Scientists <u>discovered</u> some smart mammals. _____

2. The mammals <u>live</u> in the ocean.   _____

3. Many dolphins <u>learned</u> tricks.   _____

4. Scientists <u>will study</u> dolphins more.   _____

Directions Write the verb in ( ) that correctly completes each sentence.

5. These dolphins live at the sea park, and they (perform, performed) each day.

   _____

6. A few minutes ago, a dolphin (leaps, leaped) out of the water.

   _____

7. Tomorrow the dolphins (invented, will invent) a new trick.

   _____

8. In next week's show, a dolphin (tossed, will toss) a ball into a net.

   _____

9. Yesterday the dolphins (played, play) happily with their trainers.

   _____

10. I (enjoyed, will enjoy) dolphins in the future.

    _____

11. In yesterday's show, a dolphin (pushed, will push) a ball across the pool.

    _____

12. People watch the dolphins, and then they (clapped, clap) loudly.

    _____

Irregular Verbs

Directions Choose the correct form of the irregular verb in ( ) to complete each sentence. Write the verb.

1. Mom had (gave, given) me ice water to drink. _____

2. That ice cube (begun, began) as water. _____

3. The rainwater had (run, ran) into the street. _____

4. I (saw, seen) water turn to gas. _____

5. It (took, taken) a short time on a hot day. _____

Directions Write each sentence. Use the correct past form of the verb in ( ).

6. Juan (do) a report on water.

_____

_____

7. He (find) out about conservation.

_____

_____

8. We have all (take) long showers.

_____

_____

9. We have (see) trash in lakes and rivers.

_____

_____

10. We (think) Juan's study was great.

_____

_____

Grammar and Writing Practice Book

Singular and Plural Pronouns

Directions Write the pronoun in each sentence.

1. Have you seen people fly over the ocean? _____

2. They are parasailing. _____

3. Eddie has a parachute, and it is attached to a boat. _____

4. He flies high over the beach. _____

5. It is a strange way to fly! _____

6. Sarah drives the boat, and she goes fast. _____

7. People cheer, but Eddie can't hear them. _____

8. Sarah gives him a signal. _____

9. Eddie was watching her. _____

10. Will Eddie parasail with me? _____

Directions Write *S* if the underlined pronoun is singular. Write *P* if it is plural.

11. Some people use big kites, and they jump off a high hill. _____

12. The kites carry them through the air. _____

13. Janet jumps, and she glides through the air. _____

14. All of us must take lessons before flying. _____

15. I guess people will invent even more ways to fly. _____

16. Maybe we can think of a new way. _____

17. Dan has an idea, and I like it. _____

18. He will invent a rocket pack. _____

19. Sharon is worried, and Mom agrees with her. _____

20. Dan will try, and I will help him. _____

Subject and Object Pronouns

Direction Write *SP* if the underlined pronoun is a subject pronoun. Write *OP* if it is an object pronoun.

Name _____

1. <u>I</u> visited one of the hottest places in the world. _____

2. <u>We</u> went to Death Valley in the summer. _____

3. The hot sun dazzled <u>us</u>. _____ .

4. We took plenty of water for Robert and <u>them</u>. _____

5. <u>They</u> took pictures of the desert plants. _____

Directions Choose the correct pronoun to complete each sentence. Write the sentence.

6. My family and (me, I) visited the Grand Canyon.

_____

_____

7. (We, Us) looked down one mile at the canyon's bottom.

_____

_____

8. The canyon's colors surprised Jack and (me, I).

_____

_____

9. Dad and (he, him) rafted on the river at the bottom of the canyon.

_____

_____

10. Later (they, them) hiked in the park.

_____

_____

© Pearson Education, Inc. 3

Possessive Pronouns

Directions Write the possessive pronouns in the sentences.

1. Uncle Rick has valuable rocks on his ranch. _____

2. Aunt Julie makes her jewelry with the stones. _____

3. She likes their blue color. _____

4. Our gifts were made from her purple stones. _____

5. Mine is a necklace, and hers is a pin. _____

Directions Choose the possessive pronoun in ( ) that could replace the underlined words in each sentence. Write the sentence.

6. I bought a ring, and the ring's stones are green. (their, its)

   _____

   _____

7. The artists showed us the artists' best jewelry. (his, their)

   _____

   _____

8. The green stones are the color of Laura's eyes. (hers, her)

   _____

   _____

9. Are these earrings the earrings you own? (his, yours)

   _____

   _____

10. My necklace is ruby, and Jen's necklace is turquoise. (hers, yours)

    _____

    _____

© Pearson Education, Inc. 3

Name _____

Contractions

Directions Write the contraction in each sentence. Then write the word or words that make up the contraction.

1. You can't win the race without training.

_____

2. These are Olympic athletes, and they're training many hours each week.

_____

3. She's a great swimmer.

_____

4. She didn't know swimming was so challenging.

_____

5. Maybe you'll become a swimmer too.

_____

Directions Write the contraction for the underlined words.

6. You <u>will not</u> believe Gertrude Ederle's strength and will power.

_____

7. She <u>could not</u> have crossed the English Channel without them.

_____

8. The Channel is wide, and <u>it is</u> stormy.

_____

9. Many swimmers have tried to swim the Channel, and <u>they have</u> given up.

_____

10. Gertrude Ederle was a great swimmer, and <u>she is</u> my role model.

_____

Grammar and Writing Practice Book

Prepositions

Directions Write the preposition in each sentence.

1. The eagle held a fish in its feet. _____

2. The fish was for the baby eagles. _____

3. The eagle's nest was high above the lake. _____

4. The baby eagles' cries filled the air of the forest. _____

5. The mother eagle landed on the big nest. _____

Directions Write the prepositional phrase in each sentence. Underline the preposition.

6. These eagles live in Florida.

_____

7. They make their homes along the marshes.

_____

8. They lay their eggs during the winter.

_____

9. The mother bird stays with the eggs.

_____

10. The father bird gets food from the water.

_____

11. He drops it into the babies' mouths.

_____

12. The babies will leave the nest before summer.

_____

Name _____

Adjectives and Articles

Directions Circle each article. Underline each adjective.

1. Once, the word *kimono* referred to all clothes in Japan.

2. Then a new piece of clothing was invented.

3. People called the loose outfit a kimono.

4. They loved the bright, colorful kimonos.

5. A kimono was an outfit for both men and women.

Directions Choose the article in ( ) that correctly completes each sentence. Write the sentence.

6. Kimonos had (a, an) advantage over other clothes.

_____

_____

7. On (a, an) winter day, people could wear many layers of kimonos.

_____

_____

8. Around 1900, (a, the) people of Japan began wearing styles from Europe and America.

_____

_____

9. Now, people might wear kimonos for (a, the) wedding.

_____

_____

10. Kimonos are (a, an) enchanting sight at parties and festivals.

_____

_____

Adjectives That Compare

Directions Underline the adjectives that compare in the sentences.

1. I have the friendliest grandparents in the world.

2. Grandpa is the busiest man in town.

3. He is older than many of his neighbors.

4. No one is nicer than Grandma.

5. I have the tastiest meals at her house.

Directions Choose the adjective in ( ) that correctly completes each sentence. Write the sentence.

6. Abuelito's life was (easier, easiest) in Texas than in Mexico.

_____

_____

7. Grandpa's stories are (longer, longest) than Abuelito's.

_____

_____

8. The family sailed on the (bigger, biggest) ship in Europe.

_____

_____

9. It was (safer, safest) than a trip in a covered wagon.

_____

_____

10. My grandparents tell the (finer, finest) stories in the world.

_____

_____

Adverbs

Directions Underline the adverbs in the sentences.

1. Luis's family recently moved to a new place.

2. Luis excitedly moved his things into his new room.

3. Next he went to meet his new neighbors.

4. Yesterday Luis saw his new school.

5. He soon got to know the new neighborhood.

Directions Choose the correct word in ( ) to complete each new sentence. Write the new sentence.

6. Maria (sudden, suddenly) felt homesick for her old school.

_____

_____

7. (Usual, Usually), Maria enjoyed meeting new people.

_____

_____

8. She sat (quietly, quiet) in class all day.

_____

_____

9. Some girls (cheerful, cheerfully) asked Maria to play.

_____

_____

10. She (quick, quickly) felt better.

_____

_____

Adverbs That Compare

Directions Underline the adverb that compares in each sentence.

1. Bread bakes longer than biscuits do.

2. The big oven heats more quickly than the other ovens.

3. Of all the breads, the banana bread will be done soonest.

4. Mrs. Stone kneads dough harder than Kelly does.

5. Of all the neighbors, Mrs. Lopez works most slowly.

Directions Choose the correct word in ( ) to complete each sentence. Write the new sentence.

6. Of all the girls, Jo learned (more quickly, most quickly) how to bake breads.

_____

_____

7. She worked (hard, hardest) of all on her tomato bread.

_____

_____

8. Everyone eats her pumpkin bread (faster, fastest) than any other bread.

_____

_____

9. Uncle Dan compliments Jo (more frequently, most frequently) than I do.

_____

_____

10. Jo stays in the kitchen (longer, longest) than Mom.

_____

_____

Name _____

Conjunctions

Directions Write the conjunction in each sentence.

1. Would you rather visit the city or the country on your trip? _____

2. You can ride horses and have picnics in the country.   _____

3. The country is quiet, but it is interesting.   _____

4. In the city, you can go to museums and cafés.   _____

5. You can ride in buses, trains, or taxis.   _____

Directions Choose the conjunction in ( ) that best completes each sentence. Write the sentence.

6. We went to the museum (but, and) saw all kinds of art.

_____

_____

7. We saw paintings of people (and, but) buildings.

_____

_____

8. Most sculptures stand on the floor, (or, but) some hang from the ceiling.

_____

_____

9. Did you like the paintings (but, or) the sculptures better?

_____

_____

10. My trip to the museum was educational (but, or) tiring.

_____

_____

Grammar and Writing Practice Book

Capital Letters

Directions If a sentence has capitalization mistakes, write correctly the words that should have capital letters. If a sentence has no capitalization mistakes, write *C*.

1. In may of 2005, my family flew to Paris, France.

   _____

2. On tuesday I visited the Eiffel Tower. _____

3. The Eiffel Tower was designed by Alexandre Gustave Eiffel.

   _____

4. The frame of the Statue of Liberty in new york was also designed by mr. Eiffel.

   _____

5. Next september, mrs. Austin will take us to see the Statue of Liberty.

   _____

Directions Write the sentences. Use capital letters correctly.

6. On independence day, Mom called philadelphia.

   _____

7. On martin luther king, jr., day in january, we went to the Washington Monument.

   _____

   _____

8. mr. and mrs. pines drove to plymouth, massachusetts, for thanksgiving.

   _____

   _____

9. Dad stopped at Mount Rushmore last memorial day.

   _____

   _____

10. On presidents' day in february, Sam visited the Lincoln Memorial.

    _____

    _____

Abbreviations

Directions Write each sentence correctly. Use correct capitalization and periods for abbreviations.

1. On nice days, dr Chin and mr Lee meet at the park.

_____

_____

2. On Monday, dr Chin brought his son c j and his dog.

_____

_____

3. Mr and mrs. Lau were at the park also.

_____

_____

4. They had seen ms Parks and d w Cho there on Saturday.

_____

_____

5. People brought their birds and cages to l. k. Williams Park.

_____

_____

Directions Write each telephone message. Correct mistakes in initials and abbreviations.

6. j b Logan called: got your order. _____

7. mr Logan, 6 parakeets, jan 10 _____

8. Pick up fri, jan 12 _____

9. ms Ryan's parakeet, p j _____

10. Got bird wed, dec 10 _____

Combining Sentences

Directions Combine each pair of sentences into a compound sentence. Use a comma and the conjunction in ( ).

1. Our class painted a mural. We worked very hard on it. (and)

_____

_____

2. We had never painted a mural. It looks great. (but)

_____

_____

3. Shall I tell you about the mural? Would you like to see it? (or)

_____

_____

Directions Combine each pair of sentences. Use the underlined words or a form of the underlined words only once in your new sentence.

4. <u>Lewis and Clark</u> sailed up the Missouri River. <u>Lewis and Clark</u> crossed the Rocky Mountains.

_____

_____

5. <u>The land</u> was a wilderness. <u>The land</u> had not been carefully explored.

_____

_____

6. Lewis <u>kept a journal of the trip</u>. Clark <u>kept a journal of the trip</u>.

_____

Name _____

Commas

Directions Fix the comma errors in the sentences in the letter. If a sentence does not have a comma error, write *C*.

1. Dear Thomas,

_____

2. I saw something wonderful and I had to tell you.

_____

3. I saw millions of yellow blue and orange butterflies.

_____

4. The palm, pine, and fruit trees were full of butterflies.

_____

5. Your friend
Justin

_____

Directions Write each sentence. Add commas where they are needed.

6. We took a trip to the rain forest on June 23 2005.

_____

7. We hiked climbed and rested in the forest.

_____

8. We saw incredible plants birds and insects.

_____

9. On the ground were fire ants harvester ants and army ants.

_____

10. The ants looked dangerous but they left us alone.

_____

Grammar and Writing Practice Book

Quotations

Directions Write *C* if a sentence is correct. If it is not correct, make the corrections that are needed.

1. Maria said, "I can have an adventure.   _____

2. I will ride a horse to the city! she exclaimed.   _____

3. "I will become a famous musician," Maria said. _____

4. "Can you play a flute? Juan asked.   _____

5. "No, but I can sing," Maria answered.   _____

Directions Write each sentence. Add a comma and quotation marks where they are needed.

6. Maria's mother asked What did you see on your journey?

_____

_____

7. I saw a clown, a horse, and a flute player Maria answered.

_____

_____

8. Maria's mother asked How long was your trip?

_____

_____

9. Maria replied I went a thousand miles, and I was gone a thousand days.

_____

_____

10. I'm so glad you came back! Maria's mother exclaimed.

_____

_____

Standardized Test Practice

Language Test

Read the passage. Decide which type of mistake, if any, appears in each underlined section. Mark the letter of your answer.

Did you ever have <u>a great idea for a business.</u> Last summer
(1)

<u>my friend corey and I</u> started a pet-sitting business. <u>Soon had</u>
(2)

<u>three customers.</u> We cared for a goldfish, <u>a gray cat, and a little</u>
(3)   (4)

<u>poodel.</u> Each day we walked the poodle, let the cat out of the

<u>Smiths house,</u> and fed the fish. We just hoped we didn't get
(5)

mixed up. We didn't want to let the fish out of the house or <u>put</u>

<u>a leash on the cat!</u>
(6)

---

1. A Spelling

   B Capitalization

   C Punctuation

   D No mistake

2. F Spelling

   G Capitalization

   H Punctuation

   J No mistake

3. A Incorrect plural noun

   B Incorrect possessive noun

   C Missing sentence part

   D No mistake

4. F Spelling

   G Capitalization

   H Punctuation

   J No mistake

5. A Incorrect plural noun

   B Incorrect possessive noun

   C Missing sentence part

   D No mistake

6. F Spelling

   G Capitalization

   H Punctuation

   J No mistake

ame _____

Units 1 and 2

TEST PRACTICE

Writing Test

Read the paragraph and answer questions 1–4.

> (1) You can easily make a pretty flower arrangement. (2) Get several flowers such as tulips or roses. (3) Your parents might let you pick flowers from your yard, or you can buy them from the supermarket. (4) Fill a vase with cool water. (5) Cut at least one inch from the stem of each flower. (6) Arrange the flowers in kind of a pattern or something so the shapes and colors look pleasing. (7) Put your flowers in a place where everyone can enjoy them!

1. Which time-order word would be best to begin sentence 4?

 A Yesterday

 B Next

 C Third

 D Finally

2. Which sentence is the best revision of sentence 6?

 F Arrange the flowers in kind of a pattern so the shapes and colors look pleasing.

 G Arrange the flowers in kind of a pattern or something.

 H Arrange the flowers.

 J Arrange the flowers so the shapes and colors look pleasing.

3. Which word would be best to replace *Put* in sentence 7?

 A Place

 B Display

 C Lay down

 D Toss

4. What is the purpose of this paragraph?

 F to persuade readers to take an action

 G to explain how to do something

 H to make readers laugh

 J to give readers important facts

Grammar and Writing Practice Book

Name _____

Language Test

Read the passage. Decide which type of mistake, if any, appears in each underlined section. Mark the letter of your answer.

> Glacier National Park and Yellowstone National Park are
>
> both beautifull outdoor places. Glacier National Park has high
>   (1)   (2)
>
> mountains and valleys of wildflowers. You'll found lakes as
>   (3)
>
> clear as glass there. Yellowstone's mountains arent as high, but
>   (4)
>
> the park has many wild animals, such as elk and bison. Smaller
>
> animals and them roam freely. Both parks gives visitors many
>   (5)   (6)
>
> sights to enjoy.

1. A Spelling

   B Capitalization

   C Punctuation

   D No mistake

2. F Spelling

   G Capitalization

   H Punctuation

   J No mistake

3. A Incorrect verb use

   B Incorrect contraction use

   C Incorrect pronoun use

   D No mistake

4. F Incorrect verb use

   G Incorrect contraction use

   H Incorrect pronoun use

   J No mistake

5. A Incorrect verb use

   B Incorrect contraction use

   C Incorrect pronoun use

   D No mistake

6. F Incorrect verb use

   G Incorrect contraction use

   H Incorrect pronoun use

   J No mistake

Name _____

Writing Test

Read the paragraph and answer questions 1–4.

(1) Annie Smith Peck was an unusual woman. (2) In the 1800s, women did not climb mountains. (3) But Annie had already gone up huge mountains in Europe and North America from 1895–1897. (4) Men also climbed these mountains. (5) She wanted to reach the peak of the highest mountain in Peru. (6) She made many tries over the next few years but had to turn back each time. (7) In 1908, Peck safely reached the highest point in Peru.

1. Which sentence should be left out of this paragraph?

   A Sentence 1

   B Sentence 2

   C Sentence 4

   D Sentence 5

2. Which word would be best to replace *gone* in sentence 3?

   F scurried

   G climbed

   H strolled

   J got

3. Which time-order word would best begin sentence 5?

   A First

   B Once

   C Second

   D Next

4. Which of the following sentences has sensory details that could be used for elaboration after sentence 7?

   F Annie climbed nearly 20,000 feet.

   G The mountain is about 100 miles from the Pacific coast.

   H Peck fought icy slopes and blasting winds on the way down the mountain.

   J The Matterhorn has an unusual pointed peak.

© Pearson Education, Inc.3

156 Units 3–4   **Grammar and Writing Practice Book**

Language Test

Read the passage. Decide which type of mistake, if any, appears in each underlined section. Mark the letter of your answer.

> Cooking dishes from other countries is <u>a great way to learn</u>
>
> <u>about other culchures.</u> You can start with tacos, <u>a Mexican dish.</u>
> (1)   (2)
>
> Pizza, one of the most popular Italian dishes, <u>makes a delicious</u>
>   (3)
>
> <u>friday night meal.</u> Mom makes seafood stews from both Spain
>
> and Portugal, <u>but the one from Spain is the tastiest of the two.</u>
>   (4)
>
> You don't need to travel <u>to create a international adventure.</u>
>   (5)
>
> Just cook delicious foods from around the world <u>for you your</u>
>
> <u>family and your friends.</u>
>   (6)

1. **A** Spelling
   B Capitalization
   C Punctuation
   D No mistake

2. **F** Spelling
   G Capitalization
   H Punctuation
   J No mistake

3. **A** Spelling
   B Capitalization
   C Punctuation
   D No mistake

4. **F** Incorrect article use
   G Incorrect adjective use
   H Incorrect adverb use
   J No mistake

5. **A** Incorrect article use
   B Incorrect verb use
   C Incorrect adverb use
   D No mistake

6. **F** Spelling
   G Capitalization
   H Punctuation
   J No mistake

Writing Test

Read the paragraph and answer questions 1–4.

> (1) Martin Luther King, Jr., fought for the freedom of all people. (2) King thought African Americans should have the same rights as other Americans. (3) However, he did not believe in using violence to gain rights. (4) He led peaceful protests. (5) He led a march in Washington that included about 250,000 people. (6) In his speech that day, King told of his dream that all people would finally join hands and sing, "Free at last!"

1. Which would be the best elaboration for sentence 4?

A For example, black and white protesters staged "sit-ins" in places where blacks were not allowed.

B A peaceful protest doesn't have fighting and stuff.

C President Johnson signed the Voting Rights Act to help African Americans vote safely in 1965.

D Many high school and college students attended protests.

2. Which adjective would be the best choice to describe *march* in sentence 5?

F big

G remarkable

H greatest

J interesting

3. Which is the best paraphrase of the paragraph?

A Martin Luther King, Jr., did not believe in violence.

B Martin Luther King, Jr., told of his dream that all people would be free at last.

C About 250,000 people attended a march in Washington.

D Martin Luther King, Jr., used many peaceful methods to help all Americans gain equal rights.

4. What method does the writer use for the conclusion of the paragraph?

F Sum up the main idea.

G Ask a question.

H Use a quotation.

J End with an opinion.

Grammar and Writing Practice Book

Unit Writing Lessons

Name _____

Notes for a Personal Narrative

Directions Fill in the graphic organizer with information about the event or experience that you plan to write about.

Summary

What happened? _____

When? _____

Where? _____

Who was there? _____

Details

Beginning

Middle

End

Grammar and Writing Practice Book

Name _____

Words That Tell About *You*

Directions How did you feel about your experience at the beginning, middle, and end? Choose one or two words from the word bank to describe each part of your experience. Then add details that *show* readers each feeling.

worried	excited	proud	sad
disappointed	embarrassed	satisfied	curious
puzzled	anxious	delighted	upset

Beginning _____

_____

_____

_____

Middle _____

_____

_____

_____

End _____

_____

_____

_____

Name _____

Elaboration
Combine Sentences

When you write, you can elaborate by combining short, choppy simple sentences to make compound sentences. The two sentences you combine must make sense together. You can combine the sentences using the word *and, but,* or *or.*

Directions Use the word in ( ) to combine the two sentences. Remember to capitalize the first word of the new sentence and to replace the first period with a comma.

1. (but) Many huge weeds grew in the garden. I pulled each weed out.

_____

_____

2. (and) The job was hard. It took me all afternoon.

_____

_____

3. (or) Pull out the weed's root. The weed will grow back.

_____

_____

4. (and) I earned five dollars. I felt good about my hard work.

_____

_____

5. (but) I was tired. The garden looked great.

_____

_____

Name _____

Self-Evaluation Guide
Personal Narrative

Directions Think about the final draft of your personal narrative. Then rate yourself on a score of from 4 to 1 (4 is the highest) on each writing trait. After you fill out the chart, answer the questions.

Writing Traits	4	3	2	1
Focus/Ideas				
Organization/Paragraphs				
Voice				
Word Choice				
Sentences				
Conventions				

1. What is the best part of your personal narrative?

_____

_____

_____

_____

2. Write one thing you would change about this personal narrative if you had the chance to write it again.

_____

_____

_____

Name _____

How-to Chart

Directions Fill in the graphic organizer with information about your project.

Task _____

Materials _____

Introduction _____

_____

_____

_____

Steps _____

_____

_____

_____

Conclusion _____

_____

_____

_____

Name _____

Time-Order Words

Directions Add a time-order word to each of the five steps below. Write each sentence. Then add a final sentence using a time-order word. Tell what you could do with the flowers.

1. Find a pretty vase.

_____

_____

2. Pick some wildflowers from a field.

_____

_____

3. Put water in the vase.

_____

_____

4. Place the flowers in the water.

_____

_____

5. Arrange the flowers in an attractive pattern.

_____

_____

6. _____

_____

Name _____

Elaboration

Vivid Words

When you write, you can elaborate by using vivid, precise words. For example, you can use specific common nouns and proper nouns.

General Words   Watch that kite <u>go</u> in the <u>air</u>.
Precise Words   Watch that kite <u>soar</u> up in the <u>clouds</u>.

Directions Replace each underlined word with a vivid, precise word. Write each sentence.

1. Cut paper for your kite in a <u>shape</u>.

_____

_____

2. <u>Make</u> your kite a <u>good</u> <u>color</u>.

_____

_____

3. <u>Put</u> some sticks on your kite.

_____

_____

4. <u>Put</u> your kite high in the air.

_____

_____

5. <u>Use</u> your kite with some <u>people</u>.

_____

_____

Name _____

Self-Evaluation Guide
How-to Report

Directions Think about the final draft of your how-to report. Then rate yourself on a scale of from 4 to 1 (4 is the highest) on each writing trait. After you fill out the chart, answer the questions.

Writing Traits	4	3	2	1
Focus/Ideas				
Organization/Paragraphs				
Voice				
Word Choice				
Sentences				
Conventions				

1. What is the best part of your how-to report?

   _____

   _____

   _____

   _____

2. Write one thing you would change about this how-to report if you had the chance to write it again.

   _____

   _____

   _____

   _____

Name _____

Compare/Contrast T-Chart

Directions Write a topic sentence for your compare and contrast essay. Use the T-chart to compare and contrast two things in nature. Write a conclusion sentence.

Topic Sentence _____

_____

Similarities	Differences

Conclusion Sentence _____

_____

Name _____

Words That Compare and Contrast

Directions The words in the box signal that two things are alike or different. Write two sentences that explain how your two topics are alike. Use words from the box. Then write two sentences that explain how your two topics are different. Use words from the box.

Words That Signal Similarity	Words That Signal Difference
and	but
also	however
too	on the other hand
as well	

How the two things are alike

1. _____

_____

2. _____

_____

How the two things are different

1. _____

_____

2. _____

_____

Name _____

Elaboration

Main and Helping Verbs

> You can use helping verbs with main verbs to show that something happens at a specific time.
>
> | | |
> |---|---|
> | **General** | Rain helps the flowers grow. |
> | **More Specific** | Rain will help the flowers grow. |
> | | Rain has (*or* had) helped the flowers grow. |

Directions Add a helping verb to the underlined verb in each sentence. Show that each action happened at the time shown in ( ). You may have to change the form of the main verb. Write each new sentence.

1. The weather <u>turns</u> cold in winter. (future)

_____

2. Snow <u>covers</u> the roofs and trees. (past)

_____

3. Flowers <u>bloom</u> early next spring. (future)

_____

4. The sun <u>helps</u> things grow. (past)

_____

5. The trees <u>drop</u> their leaves already this fall. (past)

_____

6. Wind <u>scatters</u> the leaves around the yard. (future)

_____

© Pearson Education, Inc. 3

Name _____

Self-Evaluation Guide
Compare and Contrast Essay

Directions Think about the final draft of your compare and contrast essay. Then rate yourself on a scale of from 4 to 1 (4 is the highest) on each writing trait. After you fill out the chart, answer the questions.

Writing Traits	4	3	2	1
Focus/Ideas				
Organization/Paragraphs				
Voice				
Word Choice				
Sentences				
Conventions				

1. What is the best part of your compare and contrast essay?

   _____

   _____

   _____

   _____

2. Write one thing you would change about this compare and contrast essay if you had the chance to write it again.

   _____

   _____

   _____

   _____

Name _____

Story Chart

Directions Fill in the graphic organizer with information about your story.

Title

Characters

Setting

Events

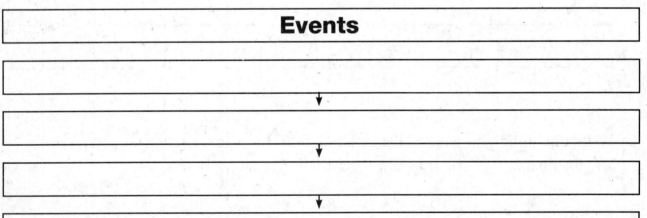

Solution

Name _____

Write a Strong Story Opener

> Make the first sentence of your story grab your readers' attention. Below are some different kinds of story openers.

Directions Write an attention-grabbing opening sentence (based on your characters, setting, and plot) using each idea. Use one of the sentences to begin your story.

1. **Ask a question.** (*Example: Have you ever heard of a 10-year-old composer?*)

   _____

2. **Use an exclamation.** (*Example: What a talented boy Jeffrey Jackson was!*)

   _____

3. **Use a sound word.** (*Example: Whoosh! Traffic sped past Jeffrey.*)

   _____

4. **Hint at the ending.** (*Example: As Jeffrey walked to school that day, he never imagined being on a stage in front of hundreds of people.*)

   _____

   _____

5. **Appeal to the senses.** (*Example: As lights glared in his eyes and applause thundered in his ears, Jeffrey shook the conductor's sweaty hand.*)

   _____

   _____

6. **Set the scene.** (*Example: The audience waited breathlessly as the conductor raised his baton before the orchestra.*)

   _____

   _____

Name _____

Elaboration
Prepositional Phrases

You can use prepositional phrases to add specific details to your story. For example, a prepositional phrase can tell where or when something happens or is located.

General	David climbed a mountain.
More Specific	David climbed a mountain near his home.

Directions Add one or more prepositional phrases to each sentence to make it more specific. Write your sentence.

1. David bought special boots.

_____

_____

2. The weather can be very cold and snowy.

_____

_____

3. Some skilled climbers went with David.

_____

_____

4. David had food and water.

_____

_____

Grammar and Writing Practice Book

Name _____

Self-Evaluation Guide
Story

Directions Think about the final draft of your story. Then rate yourself on a scale of from 4 to 1 (4 is the highest) on each writing trait. After you fill out the chart, answer the questions.

Writing Traits	4	3	2	1
Focus/Ideas				
Organization/Paragraphs				
Voice				
Word Choice				
Sentences				
Conventions				

1. What is the best part of your story?

   _____

   _____

   _____

   _____

2. Write one thing you would change about this story if you had the chance to write it again.

   _____

   _____

   _____

   _____

Name _____

Persuasion Chart

Directions Fill in the graphic organizer with ideas for the introduction, supporting reasons, and conclusion in your persuasive letter.

Introduction: State your opinion or goals.

↓

First reason

↓

Second reason

↓

Third reason (most important)

↓

Conclusion

© Pearson Education, Inc. 3

Name _____

Use Persuasive Words

> **Persuasive words** convince readers to take an action or agree with the writer's opinion. Here are some different kinds of persuasive words:
>
> **Words that state that an action is necessary:** *should, must, important*
> **Words that compare:** *best, most delicious, most important*
> **Words that describe positive traits:** *educational, healthful, safe, effective*

Directions Write sentences for your persuasive letter. Use the kind of persuasive word shown. Underline your persuasive words.

1. Word that states that an action is necessary

_____

_____

2. Word that compares

_____

_____

3. Word that describes positive traits

_____

_____

4. Any kind of persuasive word

_____

_____

Name _____

Elaboration

Specific Adverbs

> You have learned that adverbs tell about verbs. They can tell **when** (*soon, often*), **where** (*outside, here*), or **how** (*excitedly, carefully, hungrily*) something happens. You can use adverbs to make your letter more specific and persuasive.
>
> | | |
> |---|---|
> | **General** | She looked at the photographs of Puerto Rico. |
> | **More Specific** | She looked closely at the photographs of Puerto Rico. |

Directions Add an adverb to each sentence to make it more specific. Write the new sentence.

1. Japanese people ____ wear kimonos for special occasions.

   _____

   _____

2. Sam ate the big plate of spaghetti ____.

   _____

   _____

3. Tourists in China ____ walk on the Great Wall.

   _____

   _____

4. You must wrap those Mexican vases ____.

   _____

   _____

Name _____

Self-Evaluation Guide
Persuasive Letter

Directions Think about the final draft of your letter. Then rate yourself on a scale of from 4 to 1 (4 is the highest) on each writing trait. After you fill out the chart, answer the questions.

Writing Traits	4	3	2	1
Focus/Ideas				
Organization/Paragraphs				
Voice				
Word Choice				
Sentences				
Conventions				

1. What is the best part of your persuasive letter?

   _____

   _____

   _____

   _____

2. Write one thing you would change about this letter if you had the chance to write it again.

   _____

   _____

   _____

Name _____

K-W-L Chart

Directions Fill out this K-W-L chart to help you organize your ideas.

Topic _____

What I <u>K</u>now	What I <u>W</u>ant to Know	What I <u>L</u>earned

Controlling Question _____

Name _____

Topic and Detail Sentences

A topic sentence tells the main idea of a paragraph. Detail sentences give supporting facts, descriptions, and examples about the main idea.

Directions Decide how you will organize your paragraphs. Then write a topic sentence and supporting details for each paragraph.

Paragraph 1

Topic Sentence _____

Detail Sentences _____

_____

_____

_____

Paragraph 2

Topic Sentence _____

Detail Sentences _____

_____

_____

_____

Paragraph 3

Topic Sentence _____

Detail Sentences _____

_____

_____

_____

Paragraph 4

Topic Sentence _____

Detail Sentences _____

_____

_____

Name _____

Elaboration

Combine Sentences

When you **combine sentences,** you join two sentences that are about the same topic. You make them into one sentence.

- You can join two simple sentences and make a compound sentence. Add a comma and a conjunction such as *and, but,* or *or.*
- You can combine two sentences that have the same subject or the same predicate.

Directions Use the word in ( ) to combine each pair of sentences. Remember to add a comma.

1. There are many monuments in Washington. Many people visit them. (and)

   _____

   _____

2. Some monuments honor presidents. Others honor soldiers and other ordinary people. (but)

   _____

   _____

Directions Combine the sentences. Use the underlined words only once in your new sentence.

3. Some monuments <u>are made of white marble</u>. Some statues <u>are made of white marble</u>.

   _____

   _____

Name _____

Self-Evaluation Guide
Research Report

Directions Think about the final draft of your report. Then rate yourself on a scale of from 4 to 1 (4 is the highest) on each writing trait. After you fill out the chart, answer the questions.

Writing Traits	4	3	2	1
Focus/Ideas				
Organization/Paragraphs				
Voice				
Word Choice				
Sentences				
Conventions				

1. What is the best part of your research report?

_____

_____

_____

_____

2. Write one thing you would change about this research report if you had the chance to write it again.

_____

_____

_____